ISBN 978-1-330-43443-7
PIBN 10033286

FB &c Ltd, Dalton House, 60 Windsor Avenue, London, SW19 2RR.
Company number 08720141. Registered in England and Wales.

For support please visit www.forgottenbooks.com

The Philosophy of Self-Help

An Application of Practical Psychology to Daily Life

By

Stanton Davis Kirkham

Author of "The Ministry of Beauty," "Where Dwells the Soul Serene," "In the Open," etc.

God helps them that help themselves

G. P. Putnam's Sons
New York and London
The Knickerbocker Press
1912

The Knickerbocker Press, New York

PREFACE

SOME of the ideas which underlie mental therapeutics have become permanent constituents of modern thought, as recently discovered chemical elements are permanent factors in chemical science. I purpose here to give an outline of these thought elements of metaphysics and psychology, to systematize their essential principles and to show their practical bearing upon the art of living, of mind and character building, whereby the individual, through recognition and application, may develop for himself a more rounded character, a more efficient mind, a healthier body, and hence come to live a more effective, a more beautiful, and a happier life. This he will do for himself in the ratio that he first perceives and then applies the truth. It is, therefore, with the paramount desire of helping others to help themselves that this book is written.

S. D. K.

CONTENTS

All that we are is the result of what we have thought: it is founded on our thoughts, it is made up of our thoughts. If a man speaks or acts with an evil thought, pain follows him, as the wheel follows the foot of him who draws the carriage.

All that we are is the result of what we have thought: it is founded on our thoughts, it is made up of our thoughts. If a man speaks or acts a pure thought, happiness follows him, like a shadow that never leaves him.

Whatever a hater may do to a hater, or an enemy to an enemy, a wrongly-directed mind will do us greater mischief.

Not a mother, not a father will do so much, nor any other relative; a well-directed mind will do us greater service.

Let the wise man guard his thoughts, for they are difficult to perceive, very artful, and they rush wherever they list: thoughts well guarded bring happiness.

The Dhammapada.

FOREWORD

SOME fifty years ago, Quimby affirmed that disease was a false belief outwardly picturing itself in the body, and that a cure would be effected by substituting in the mind true ideas for false ones. It is probable that this was the first attempt in recent times at a practical application of the forces of the mind to the healing of the body upon the basis that physical ailments are the result of wrong-thinking or moral defection. A cure, then, was at the same time a moral regeneration, or at least a mental stimulus to right thinking: in fact this *was* the cure,—the physical benefits followed as a natural result.

Fifty years of mental healing in one phase or another have amply demonstrated that there was some truth—if not all of the truth—in Quimby's assertion. The means he employed, consciously or unconsciously, was the power of Suggestion: not random suggestion, but the suggestion of truth, of metaphysical, ethical, and spiritual principles to the mind whose disorder was revealed in the bodily disturbance. The power of suggestion is to-day generally recognised. Aside from the schools of mental healing, it has been employed in one form or another, usually as hypnotic suggestion, notably in Europe by Charcot and Bernheim and in America by Dr. Mason and others.

Whether employed in hypnosis or in normal states, suggestion is suggestion, and it is that which accomplishes the work While it is quite possible that in some cases it may be more effective during hypnosis, and Dr. Mason's experiments would seem to indicate this, hypnotism is no more to be lightly used than are anæsthetics, and only by very responsible persons. In the hands of the irresponsible it is a menace The control of another's will is to be deprecated on general principles. A consideration of hypnotism does not come within the scope of the present work wherein we shall confine ourselves to normal suggestion which from one source or another, consciously or unconsciously, is persistently playing upon every mind. When this mental force is systematically controlled and directed upon principles

—upon metaphysical and spiritual truths—the mind is strengthened, character developed, and bodily conditions improved in consequence. Effective mental action of this kind implies not alone will and intelligence to direct the thought, but first a perception of truth, and understanding of principles upon which to direct it.

Auto-suggestion is, therefore, the means of self-help with which we are here concerned: auto-suggestion with a view, that is, to mental control and development and a strengthening of the will, the results of which must become evident both in character and health.

The mind, constantly active, is generating force, which uncontrolled or misdirected works harm, as readily and as obviously as any other force ignorantly handled. Systematically and wisely directed, it is a power for good at the disposal of every man, by which he may increase his efficiency and his happiness and may assist others to do so for themselves. The working of the mind, the action of suggestion, comes wholly within the province of Psychology. That body of truth, however, upon which it is profitable to direct the mind which we must have as the subject of our thinking—philosophical religions, ethical—is but that ancient wisdom scattered through the sacred books of the world and nowhere more in evidence than in the Bible. Consonant with the teaching of Jesus, it is often at variance with the tenets of Theology.

In this book, we shall, therefore, first briefly review this body of truth—the normal field of the mind's activity. We shall then consider more at length the nature and activity of the mind itself and its relation to the body; and we shall conclude with such logical deductions and inferences as may be drawn, and such practical suggestions as may occur, with reference to mind building and character forming, through an application of the principles discussed.

In this connection it would be well to emphasise, at the outset, the important truth that all we know is necessarily through our minds; sensation, not less than perception and conception, is mental. All depends, therefore, on the quality and fitness of the mind we possess. By its means, as through a glass, we take cognisance of the world and of life. If the glass is out of focus we see a distorted image. Hence the prime necessity of wise and systematic thought-control and direction in accordance with true ideals of life and of character. Through this agency we replace error in the mind with truth, discord with harmony, and weak and sickly ideas with strong and wholesome ones.

The influence of the mind upon the body is to-day more fully recognised than the reaction of the quality of thought upon the mind itself. We are now inquiring how and why the mind effects the body. The consideration of its *modus operandi* belongs to Psychology and will in time be incorporated in that expanding science. Suggestion, telepathy, the sub-conscious, are now considered under the caption of the "New Psychology." Properly there is no new psychology; Psychology is merely, like other sciences, in process of development. We do not speak of a New Chemistry and a New Physics because new elements have been discovered and new theories accepted. Yet this would be quite as correct as to speak of a New Psychology. New lands and stars have been discovered, and, from time to time, errors are corrected in the results of former observations. So in psychology unknown fields of mental action are being explored and relations established, and it would be as absurd for psychologists to ignore these, as for geographers to treat of the world as the Phœnecians knew it. While new lands are always not the discovery of geographers or of savants, they none the less pertain to Geography and must be shown on the latest maps, provided their existence has been verified and is not merely a sailor's yarn. Discoveries in the field of psychology have not all been made by Professors of Psychology, but they must be recognised by them, whereever bonafide, and must be incorporated in that science.

Mental healing is far from lying wholly within the domain of Psychology. It rests on the foundation of metaphysics and of ethics, as the working of a machine depends on fundamental and cosmic laws relating to matter and force. As to what are true concepts and what are not, it is not for Psychology to decide and we must invoke, not Metaphysics alone, but Ethics and Philosophy. If we are to help ourselves, or others, it must be in accordance with true ideals. We must know at least cardinal facts of life, and what is more, be able to distinguish fact from appearance, truth from error.

While it is advisable to think truly and

to be just and kind because of mental and physical reactions, the ground of such thought and conduct is not mere expediency, but the love of righteousness and the love of truth, the basis of both religion and philosophy.

It is not the aim of the present work to be in any sense polemical. It rests on truths now as generally admitted by idealists as they are denied with vehemence by those still claiming to be materialists.

From a religious standpoint, it will appear unorthodox. The advanced thinker may find its point of view congenial; the ultraconservative will take exception. No attempt will be made to reconcile divergent opinions, but the sole consideration will be to state the truth—and that with due tolerance of the opinions of others. This is undertaken in the interest of no Sect, School, or Society whatsoever, but wholly in the interest of the truth itself, and with the desire of helping others to help themselves through a clearer perception of spiritual facts, a better understanding of themselves and the application of a simple and practical psychology to everyday life. It is proposed to do this in as direct, logical, and systematic manner as possible—to present in fact an outline, an elementary and practical treatise on the philosophy and psychology of daily life.

The philosophy which underlies mental healing, while not well-defined, nor as yet ever systematically enunciated, is perhaps on the whole, the most sane and the most practical of modern times. In most books on the subject the words *spirit*, *soul*, and *mind* are used indiscriminately to the confusion of the reader. They are not properly synonymous and they will here be clearly distinguished.

There is nothing new in this philosophy; it does, however, represent a great development in *practical psychology* and it is a curious fact that it has done more to advance that subject in the estimation of mankind than the most distinguished men in that science have ever been able to do. Aside from this, it is a restatement of old truths; for that matter, so is every philosophy and every religion. No system can ever again be formulated that shall not owe something to earlier ones; as no stratum of rock can ever be added to the earth's crust that shall not be composed of earlier geologic strata.

But it is not a matter of chance that it is a

restatement of particular truths and an elimination of particular errors. It is the expression of Idealism in these Times and of this People: at heart a religious movement, as well as an obstinate attempt of a practical people to divest themselves of popular fallacies and to get nearer the truth. It came into being because of the spiritual needs of this age and belongs to this age. We have however all too many divisions, religious and irreligious, philosophic and unphilosophic, upon which to hang our prejudices.

We do not, every time a new island is discovered, thereupon establish a new school of geography; and for a like reason, advance in any science belongs to that science and its benefits to all who can avail themselves of its truth.

PART I

FIRST PRINCIPLES

CHAPTER I

METAPHYSICS

IN the following review of first principles no general exposition of such large subjects as metaphysics, religion, and ethics is proposed, but the intention is merely to get at that in each which is fundamental and the consideration of which is essential to our subject—a practical one, undertaken, not for any mere speculative interest, but wholly because of its bearing upon character and health.

It is not the abstractions of metaphysics, but a true metaphysical basis for our own thinking which concerns us; not speculative philosophy but a sane philosophy of life; not the psychology of schoolmen but the practical working and efficient control of the mind. It can be shown that these subjects, far from being the mere diversion of scholars and pedants, are those which alone enable us to establish a true ground for our thinking; that as they are necessarily the basis of right-thinking, so is right-thinking in turn the foundation of health and happiness.

We shall now briefly consider some aspects of metaphysics which will aid us in defining our point of view, and which will serve as a preparation for what is to follow.

First, as to the psychology of perception; the facts are quite at variance with the fiction commonly accepted as truth. Perception of the external world is through sensation; the five senses are so many open doors through which tidings come to us from without. To the eye, come ethereal vibrations of inconceivable rapidity and of different wave lengths. To the ear come aerial vibrations of comparative slowness, varying with the pitch. Through touch, taste, and smell, we receive other modes of vibration, each appealing to the special nerve apparatus designed to receive it. When the vibration impinges upon the nerve receiver—the retina for instance—it sets up another mode of vibration in that organ which is communicated to the corresponding brain area, where it gives rise to still further activity. This final activity is interpreted by the percipient mind, and the object from which emanated the original vibration is perceived, as a red rose let us say. Again, let sound waves fall upon the ear and through a similar process the mind perceives the tolling of a bell. But the colour of the rose and the sound of the bell are purely *sensations* in the percipient mind; in the external world, until they reach the brain and are interpreted by the mind, they are *vibrations* merely. Colour and sound are in the eye and ear and not in the object, or to speak precisely, sensation is an act of consciousness. Pain is in the mind; pleasure is in the mind.

As we cannot know God directly, so neither can we know matter *per se*. All that we know, or ever can know directly of matter are the sensations to which it gives rise in the mind. This brings us to the consideration of mind and matter and I shall aim to clearly state my position in this regard: for it is a subject on which the world is always divided and in reference to which much confusion exists, the object to-day of much ill-considered speculation and unphilosophic thought.

It is indisputable that we cannot know the object in itself, but only the sensations to which it gives rise; that the outer world is both colourless and soundless, and that what we perceive as colour and sound are sensations induced in us by vibrations from without—that sensation is wholly in mind. What then does exist outside of ourselves? What is matter? It will be recalled that extreme Idealism—such as Christian Science—takes the position that all is mind and there is no such thing as matter. This ground is certainly untenable, though it is not as absurd as it appears to the unthinking or half-educated. The opposite extreme—that all is matter, and that what we call mind is merely a secretion of matter—is far more absurd. It should be remembered that, since *knowing* is itself a mental process and all we know of matter is through mind, the burden of proof rests upon the materialist and not upon the idealist. To prove the existence of matter is more difficult than to prove the existence of mind.

We know a rose by means of its form, colour, and perfume. As we have seen, these give rise to sensations which result in the perception of the rose. We have interpreted, not the rose itself however, but only those sensations induced by the rose Take away form, colour, and perfume and what remains? Nothing, says the extremist; there was nothing to begin with but your own sensations. This is one of those half-truths which so often pass for truth. What gives us these particular sensations, or any sensations, when we look at the rose? It is true the colour is in the mind and not in the object, but it is equally true that the sensation of colour in the mind is induced by a vibration from without, emanating from a something—we know not what—and that without that vibration and that unknowable something which gives rise to vibration, we would have no sensation of colour.' That something is what we call *matter*. What it is in itself we do not know: we know it only by its qualities. But whatever it may be, it is as real as the perceiving mind.

That which does not endure, and hence is properly not real but an appearance merely, is the *form* which matter assumes to us. With perfect propriety we may affirm that form has no reality, but we cannot truly so affirm of matter itself, that unknown something perceived through its multiple forms. To return to the rose—its form is constantly changing; during no two successive intervals of time is it precisely the same, though by reason of the coarseness of our vision we are unable to take note of these mutations. From the seed in the ground to the full-blown rose and thence to the soil to which its petals return, we may never truly say of the form that it *is*, but only that it is *becoming*. The idea of the rose persists as does that unknown *matter* with which it is clothed; but the form by which we perceive it, does not persist and is unreal, is a phantom shape appearing on the field of consciousness for a moment, only to vanish into nothingness.

So with the outer world, so with our own bodies; the form which they assume is unreal, the unknown and unknowable substance of which they are composed is indestructible. Used over and over again in millions of bodies and millions of worlds, it has not life of itself, but is animated by the life-force. The Spirit puts it on as a garment and casts it off again. You may tear the garment into tatters, you may burn the rags to ashes, but you have only resolved the primeval matter into some other form. Both spirit and matter are indestructible; form alone is unreal. What we call matter, then, is the object of which spirit is the subject. One implies the other. There cannot be an inside and no outside, nor an outside and no inside. Similarly there cannot be a subject with no object of perception; neither an object with no perceiving subject. The position of spiritual monism is hence the most rational and the most unassailable:—there is one eternal Substance which is both subject and object. That "eternal Substance" is God.

In this analysis, it appears that matter merely serves to give temporary form to spirit; that it has no life of itself, no sensations in itself. It does not move but is moved; it does not act but is acted upon by the life-force. The Spirit alone gives life. Let us bring this home to ourselves in the realisation that the body has no life of itself, no sensation, no intelligence. Inert, it is acted upon by the informing mind and when that is withdrawn is resolved into its elements, which are at once seized upon to enter into other temporary combinations.

One word more as to the relation of the percipient mind to the objective world: when we look at the flower, that which we really see is the flower plus the content of our own minds. Perhaps only in infancy—if then—do we positively perceive anything; in later years we *ap*perceive always. That is to say, the result of any act of perception is instantly conjoined in the mind to the "apperceiving mass"—the ideas already in the mind—and what we become conscious of is in reality the sum. This "apperceiving mass" may be very slight, it may be very vague; the more highly cultivated the mind, the more likely it is to be considerable because of the extensive association of ideas. A simple peasant, therefore, comes nearer to seeing a rose as a rose, than the naturalist, the poet, or the philosopher. In the minds of the latter it induces, together with the acts of perception, so many associative processes that the view of the object is coloured by personal experience, the play of emotion, and a scientific or a philosophic bias.

The practical bearing of the foregoing facts will be seen at once when we consider that, as all we know is through mind, much depends on the quality and fitness of the mind we possess. To look through a distorting glass is to see a distorted world; and to perceive the world with a mind out of focus is to see life all awry. To put the mind in focus that it may see life clearly as it is—fact for fact and error for error—is the object of this study. If we were to adjust a telescope we should require a knowledge of the laws of optics, and for the same reason we cannot properly regulate the mind without an understanding of those elements of philosophy which are the basis of true concepts and right-thinking.

If now we regard causation, we shall see that it is not the property of matter but of mind, for matter does not act of itself but is acted upon. The relation of the mind to the brain we shall take up in a later chapter. It is sufficient for the moment to say that idealism naturally rests on the assumption that the brain is merely the instrument of the mind, in opposition to the materialistic assertion that thought is the secretion of the brain. Recent study of the pathology of the brain has given ample proof of the validity of the idealist position, which will here be taken not as hypothesis but as fact.

The idea of mental causation is the working basis of mental healing and while it is grounded in fact, it needs some qualification. Matter is acted upon by force, and that force may be resident in the individual mind or in that aspect of the cosmic mind we call Nature. The brain has been compared by Dr. Thompson, in his study of that organ, to a violin. The violin does not play of itself; it is played upon. But the player is dependent upon his violin, no matter how great a musician he may be. So the mind uses the brain as an instrument, but if the brain fails to act normally, the mind cannot function through it.

The player is as good a violinist as ever, but he cannot manifest his talent with that violin; the mind may be clear, but it cannot function normally on the material plane with a defective instrument.

The analogy between the brain and the violin is by no means complete, and the illustration serves us no further for the simple reason that the violin is independent of the player, while the moment the thinker is dissociated from the brain, that instrument begins to disintegrate and returns to the dust from which it was fashioned. It has no life apart from the thinker who uses it. Mark the important fact that it is built up day by day, or disintegrated as the case may be, by the quality of thought indulged by the informing mind.

It may be argued that, as we cannot live without eating, therefore food is the material cause of our life. While we are dependent upon food for our expression on this plane, there is no life in food itself, but the life-force seizes upon food to build the body. The life-force is not a property of food; it is resident in universal mind and merely uses food as it uses the dust to give form to an idea. Much less can drugs be said to have life in themselves. The life-force avails itself of food as its natural building material; it does not so avail itself of drugs, unless what we name a drug is in reality a food-preparation under that name, in which case it is properly not a drug at all but a food. A mason picks up stone after stone and builds it into his wall, but if by chance he takes up a bit of rubbish, he immediately rejects it as unsuitable to his purpose—it is not building material. So the life-force uses food, but it cannot use a drug. The assumption, however, that a drug has no action whatever, apart from a belief in it, is untenable; it may or may not have a chemical reaction and this, be it remembered, is not matter acting upon itself but force acting upon matter. The assumption, on the other hand, that a drug has no *curative* action apart from belief and faith, rests on good ground and is essentially true. In any case no action takes place in the body independent of mind, conscious or subconscious. Apart from the mind the body has no existence and the mind is necessarily a factor in every change, molecular or atomic, which goes on in this its material expression.

The nature and extent of these reactions

are extremely variable and governed by psychic conditions of which at present we have little understanding. It is amply vouched for by competent witnesses that certain South Sea Islanders walk upon hot stones and are not burned; that the Hopi Indians are repeatedly bitten by rattlesnakes with fangs intact and not poisoned. In hypnosis, sweet may taste sour and sour sweet, hot water be cold and ice water hot, pain be pleasant and pleasure pain—all at the will of the agent.

In concluding this preliminary chapter, let us consider an aspect of nature in its bearing upon the individual. Nature is cosmic mind in manifestation. All manifestation is conditioned by the qualities, and the point to make here as essentially metaphysical in its relation is, that these qualities are resident in nature rather than in us, are universal, that is, and not personal. Birth and death are conditions of manifestation and whatever is born must die. If we do not wish to die, we must cease being born. But death, be it remembered, is not a cessation of the life-force, but merely its withdrawal from the form which it animated. Life and matter are eternal. It is the form alone which changes, for form has no abiding reality. All manifestation is conditioned by Time and Space. Only the Absolute—by its nature unconditioned—is free, a fact we shall be led to consider in connection with the Soul and consciousness. That which partakes of the Absolute, being unconditioned by Time, is eternal; but Eternity, far from being infinite extension of Time, means timelessness. The Eternal, therefore, is out of Time and Space, and it is the manifestation of life, not life itself, which is conditioned by them. Were philosophic acumen prized as much as business shrewdness, or did education provide us any philosophic training, we would have some assurance of these things, in place of the sophistry and shallow cynicism which take the place of thought.

That which we know as Nature and which makes itself known through the lower animals as Instinct is equally dominant in its control of our own minds in much that seems to us personal, but is, in reality, as impersonal as the winds. The wind blows over the forest and the leaves rustle; if the wind is west, they bend one way, and if it is east, they bend another. So, the sex instinct, the parental instinct, the food instinct, which are merely Nature acting upon us to do her will, pass over us like the winds, and when they come, we bend. Unlike the leaves, however, we may direct this power of Nature as it acts through us, in such a way as to conserve our own welfare; or we may misdirect it to our own sorrow.

Similarly the world-thought itself acts upon us like a species of contagion, and the unthinking are swayed, as bending grass in a storm, by the manias and epidemics of society. The process of self-help involves a clarifying of the intellect and a strengthening of the will, so that we may properly meet these unceasing forces of Nature and of the world in such a way as to react upon them to our own spiritual, intellectual, and physical advantage. The surf beats upon the shellfish on the shore, but they, in place of being crushed by its force, extract their food and the wherewithal to build their shells from the on-rushing waves.

The question of good and evil, of reality and unreality, which engages us under the head of Metaphysics, is reserved for the next chapter in order to consider it in connection with God, the essential Reality of the universe.

CHAPTER II

GOD

IT is essential we should entertain the clearest possible conception of that which we call God and of our relation to Him. To this end it may be necessary to divest ourselves of certain false ideals which serve no good purpose and are wholly unphilosophic: all conceptions of God, that is, which attribute to Him the possibility of change, or which constitute the Deity merely a magnified human being. Furthermore, we must get rid of the belief in two gods—in a power of Good and a power of Evil, forever opposed to each other. God may *not* be defined, for obviously the Infinite is not subject to definition. As a part cannot contain the whole, the finite mind can never grasp the Infinite which is God. We must, however, frame for ourselves an idea of God, nor is this necessarily a cold abstraction. A child can have no adequate idea of the content of his father's mind, or of that which makes up his character and personality, until he has attained years of discretion, perhaps not before he has become a father himself; yet he feels that his father is a loving and protecting influence, and that idea fulfils all the needs of his childhood. In this way we may postulate God to ourselves for the needs of our spiritual life, and while we do not in reality define, we establish our idea of God on a correct basis, true as far as it goes, and sufficient for our needs. Thus we truly affirm that God is Spirit, that God is Love, and this satisfies our religious idea. With equal verity we affirm that God is the Absolute and Unchangeable, the essential Reality, and this concept answers our metaphysical or philosophical demands.

When we come to consider the more practical and applied aspects of our subject, we shall see that we may speak as definitely and as concretely as of chemistry or geology or any other practical matter. But of God we can never speak thus directly, for the interpretation of the spiritual in terms of the phenomenal, of the Infinite in terms of the finite, must always of necessity lack explicitness as well as comprehensiveness. In this relation, faith is a larger element than reason. While the idea of God which we are here entertaining is perhaps as exact as any the human mind is capable of conceiving, we must, nevertheless, realise that God is not a particular concept but the ground of all concepts, not what we know, but that by which we know, not what we see but that power by which we are able to see.

An idea of a changeable God will have no part, then, in our philosophy; neither the idea of a ruler, king, or judge; nor of an absentee or extra cosmic god. All such ideas represent the grouping of the human mind in its slow evolution and are no more practical and not a whit more philosophical than the ideas of the savage. God is the underlying Reality of the Universe, forever immanent in the world. In Him we have our being; in us He has expression. Let us then henceforth think of God, not as loving, but as Love itself, not as wise, but as Wisdom itself, not as good, but as infinite and eternal Goodness. At the very outset we can entertain no more practical suggestion than that we should ennoble and clarify our idea of God; that we should make it more real, vital, and ever-present in consciousness. While our relation to God is religion, it is at the same time the most fundamental and practical relation of life. The time has passed when religion may be regarded as a matter of dogma or creeds or mere sentimentality. While God is never to be fully comprehended by the finite mind, the power of God can be *appropriated by man*. Here is the key to the whole matter—and this is practical religion. In a subsequent chapter we shall consider this relationship more at length, for not only is it the sum and substance of a rational religion but it is the root of any permanent self-help. Man is nothing without God; he is great in the ratio that he permits the divine energy and wisdom to manifest through him.

We were bred to the idea of a warring dualism, of opposing principles of Good and Evil, and the roots of this false theology are tangled in the mental and moral being of the race. It amounted to a belief in two gods—neither of them real. Its influence on the race-thought has been baneful. Upon him whose mind is still divided in the belief in two self-existent powers, the effect is weakening and confusing. There is one God, one Principle, one Reality, and one only—self-existent, absolute, eternal. One cannot too often fortify the mind with this concept, for in reality are our refuge and our strength. Abundant evil and abuse there surely are in the world but a principle of Evil, a self-existent power of Evil there is not, and such an idea must be buried in the graveyard of Superannuated Beliefs. From our ignorance, our mistakes, our selfishness, and the ignorance and selfishness of others, arise our troubles and tribulations, and source other than this there is none We mistake illusion for reality and appearance for fact. Ignorance has ever been the arch enemy of mankind, but mark that ignorance is neither a principle nor a person, but merely our deficiency in wisdom, as darkness is the absence of light, cold the absence of heat. Like children we learn our lessons and suffer the results of our mistakes and our faults, while through experience and through insight we slowly establish in our minds, truth in place of error, reality in place of illusion.

Later we shall consider that fundamental and yet little recognised fact of philosophy, that whatever we think a thing to be, that it is to us; for what we know is never the thing in itself, but our concept of it. This truth, so practical in its bearing upon the subject of self-help must receive considerable emphasis in the present inquiry. Thus the race has experienced continued harm through its belief in powers of evil and darkness; harm which came not from the supposed power, but from the belief itself We have been only theoretical monotheists; practically we have believed in a god of Evil quite as much, if not more, than in a God of Good. Let us aim now to admit the light, in the assurance that whereas light is real and active, darkness is not an entity but merely the absence of light and must disappear as the light enters; in the assurance, as well, that Good is the essential Reality of the universe and that Evil, having no source but the human mind, must vanish in presence of good, as darkness is dispersed by the sun's rays.

Fully as important as the concept of God as Love, is the postulate of metaphysics that God is the one Reality, and that all that is not God—not good in itself—is an appearance and not a reality. The appearance has that power with which human belief invests it, but no power in and of itself. God can be none other than good and there can be nothing but God. Therefore all that is *is* good. But alas there are appearances, illusions, figments—all masquerading as real, which like ghosts haunt the mind. To rid ourselves of these by seeing clearly—by seeing truth in place of error—is the problem that every man must endeavour to solve. To this end there is perhaps no better rule than that given by Emerson: "If we live truly, we shall see truly."

To let the light into a room means at the same time to dissipate the darkness; and to admit truth consciously to the mind means to overcome error in one and the same act. If we would be warm, we do not theorise about the sun but go into the sunlight. Concern yourself, not so much with what is God, but what is God to you. Take counsel with yourself as to whether the idea of good, or of evil, is uppermost in your mind. Which are you making real to yourself in your thoughts? How much are you bringing God into consciousness by thinking good and excluding thoughts of evil? Reflect that when your consciousness is wholly filled with good there is no room for its opposite, which then ceases to have even an apparent reality to you. If in the forest you perceive that a stump is a stump, you give no thought to the possibility of its being a bear; if on the other hand, you can not see clearly, you may be vexed with fears of a grizzly, though there is nothing ahead but a stump. Aim to see clearly, to see reality—God, that is—and not illusion and to hold fast to the real. Now God is Spirit, God is Truth, and God is Love, and to be spiritually minded, to love truth and to love mankind is to bring God into consciousness.

CHAPTER III

THE SOUL

PREVALENT notions about the Soul are even more vague and unphilosophic than the ideas of God. No distinction is made in common parlance, indeed it is seldom made by current writers on religious and philosophic topics, between the mere passing states of consciousness and the Soul which is that permanent spiritual being on which these states are combined. It is true that the materialists in Philosophy do not admit this. But those who are naturally committed to a spiritual point of view, ministers of the Gospel no less than exponents of the "New Thought," yet write with a vague notion of that fundamental truth upon which any spiritual philosophy must rest. In this materialistic age we have come to assume that spirit means something changeable, ephemeral, unreal, whereas the very reverse is true: the world of form, the phenomenal, is the impermanent, devoid of essential reality, while spirit is that which is alone unchangeable and real in an absolute sense.

The Church still preaches the salvation of the Soul, whereas that being the only part of us which is unchangeable, is obviously the one element which cannot possibly need salvation from anything, since it can never be better or worse, any more than a square can be more or less square. Much of this vagueness rises from confusion of terms as well as of ideas. What is generally implied by the Soul is, not the Soul at all, but merely the stream of consciousness. Nothing is more important than that we should clearly under stand this distinction, and to do this we must divest ourselves of those unphilosophic ideas in which we have grown up and which we have accepted without any thought on the subject. The basis of a real and practical mental science—of any spiritual philosophy—is the root-idea of the permanence of the Soul—the real man—in distinction to the changing consciousness. And the problem of self-help is the bringing that real man to the front, in other words, the realisation of the Soul, the bringing of the Soul into consciousness. If it were not for the Soul, this absolute and unchangeable background of consciousness, man could not be said to have any real identity at all, for consciousness itself is merely a flowing stream.

In our various states of mind we are more or less aware of an "I" who is conscious. I am now aware, for instance, that my mind is reflecting on this subject. Who is this "I" who is observing the stream of consciousness, like a spectator on the bank of a river? Who is this in the background of my idea of self? It is the self as knower—the Thinker—while the stream of consciousness at any given moment is the self as known—the empirical ego. The self as knower—the Soul—is one and unchangeable. It is that by which we are conscious; that which appropriates the various "mes" of the empirical ego and gives them a seeming identity; that upon which the states of mind are combined. This combination would be impossible were there nothing permanent upon which to combine; as you cannot have moving pictures unless there is an immovable background upon which to project them.

Our idea of self, then, is in reality dual and includes the self as knower and the self as known. Now the self as knower—the Soul—

is the subject, not the object of thought, and it is this Self which is identical in its nature with the supreme knower of the world whom we call God. As God is absolute, and out of Time and Space, so is the Soul absolute. It is one with God and inseparable from Him as the sunbeam is one with the Sun. The sunbeam has no life of its own, but partakes of the life and nature of the Sun. So does the Soul partake of the life of God and whatever may be said of God may be said of the Soul—which is God in us. It is unborn, it does not die; it is not sick, it does not suffer. It is purity and freedom, as God is purity and freedom. Fear and ignorance, which are the enemies of the world, affect the empirical ego alone and are conditions of consciousness, not of being, precisely as the fog does not obscure the Sun, though it appears to; what it really does is to obscure the Earth.

The Soul, then, is the essential reality in man; for the stream of consciousness, changing every moment, has only that apparent reality of the phenomenal universe. It seems to have an identity and to remain the same, but is in fact always passing into some other phase.

Self-knowledge implies, not a cursory knowledge of our mental states or our personal traits, but it means the perception of the Soul, the recognition of the Soul's identity with the Absolute and not with the phenomenal. The "Know thyself" of the Oracle has become a catch phrase, and its real significance is lost to view. Its inner meaning was that we should establish our identity with the Absolute and unchangeable. If, standing on the bank of a stream, you should imagine yourself to be moving onward with the current, now tossed in air, now drawn under the waters, your condition would illustrate the usual state of mind. For just so we observe the passing stream of the phenomenal and identify ourselves with it, oblivious of the fact that we—that the knower, the real man—is himself unmoved and an observer merely of the stream.

It appears that Jesus understood clearly the relation of the Soul to God which was the basis of his life and teaching and which he expressed in the saying "I and my Father are One." To assume that the idea originated with him is as unscholarly as it is absurd, for it is the fundamental doctrine of the Upanishad—an idea which dominated the religious and philosophic thought of Asia many centuries before the beginning of the Christian era. But who discovered that two and two are four; and would not the sum be four, whether any one discovered it or not? Even more vital and practical is the fact of the identity of the Soul with the Absolute. Cease to think of yourself essentially as a changeable and ephemeral creature; the body changes, consciousness is a flowing stream, but—

Thy Soul and God stand sure.

The Soul is that in us which does not suffer, nor sin, nor die; it is one with the unchangeable Truth, and the whole problem of life—in terms of philosophy—is that we should learn to identify ourselves with the Soul and not with the phenomenal world.

The Soul, as we have seen, being the eternal knower in us, is the subject of knowledge, not the object. It is, therefore, in reality, not that of which we are conscious, but that by which we have consciousness. Again it is not that which is seen but that spiritual light by which we are able to see at all.

In the following chapter we shall consider the personal self—the self as known—and it will become apparent that in the regulation of consciousness the main thing is to so clarify it that the inner light, the light of the Soul, may shine through this enveloping medium. Inasmuch as your true self is the Soul, you are already pure, wise, and free. Your life work, your schooling here, is to bring this truth into realisation.

CHAPTER IV

THE PERSONAL SELF

IF we reflect for a moment, we shall see that what we commonly regard as self is really made up of several or many selves, none of which are permanent. Some are quite evanescent, others endure for a comparatively long period; they either contract until they become nothing or expand and change until they are virtually something else. All are conditioned by age and environment. An artist has a certain idea of self which corresponds to that calling; a merchant, another; a judge, still another. Each of these is accompanied by a particular kind of self-esteem as well as a code of life more or less peculiar to itself. As a soldier one does not look at life in the same way as a clergyman, and hence has a different basis for self-esteem, or condemnation—an entirely different social self in fact. Again, in relation to our social life—our nationality, city, club, college, and society—we evolve, each for himself, a representative notion of self. In distinction to these "social selves" we have various "material selves" which are the outcome of our consciousness of the body. Strong or weak, sick or well, fat or lean, full-fed or abstemious, all have corresponding material selves. An athlete cannot possibly think of himself as a sick man, nor a bon-vivant as a lean and hungry Cassius. We have again what may be called a higher self which answers to our religious and philosophic thought. This, often enough, is only in evidence on Sunday, while at other times a professional, commercial, social, or material self is in the ascendant.

It is evident furthermore, that our ideas of self, or properly our assortment of selves, changes from year to year, and those peculiar to age are totally unlike those cherished in youth. You have little sympathy with yourself as you once were; the friends, the books, the ideals, the conduct of your earlier years may now all be abhorrent to you, and you are ready to preach against every idea you once extolled with such warmth. Much less can you understand yourself as you were when an infant and your joy in life was a rubber ring. Anon you will look back at your present self in much the same way.

Nor are we the same for two days at a time, for we have selves that correspond to our varying moods; selves which hold sway for brief periods only and immediately give way to others that may be wholly out of sympathy with them. In the normal mind, the selves are so related and banded together by a certain unity of consciousness that we slip from one to the other, as we might change our clothes, experiencing no sense of changed identity, and our friends recognise us in all this masquerade as the same man. In abnormality, however, it is different, and persons have been known to have two and even three distinct personalities, totally sundered, and having no knowledge one of the other.

The way the world looks to us at any moment depends upon which particular self is in the ascendant. If a musical self—we are quite out of harmony with a business meeting; if an harassed and preoccupied business self—then have we no heart for a quiet walk in the country, no eyes and ears for birds and flowers. Consciousness is the glass through which we look. If we are out of sorts, the world is dark: if in a cheerful frame of mind, all is bright. Evidently we must keep the glass in focus if we are to see clearly.

These various selves are merely states of mind, personal to us and of seeming permanence; in other words, they are but the stream of consciousness in a certain light and for a given time. Every state of mind is a part of our personal consciousness; the states change within consciousness, but consciousness itself is continuous, flowing onward like a river. Hence it is called by psychologists the Stream of Consciousness. While we are far from having solved all the mysteries connected with it, a number of practical truths have been arrived at, both in its working and in its relation to the body, which must engage our attention in the following pages.

In regard to our consciousness of self as a social being in distinction from the consciousness of self as body, we must observe that there are certain divine laws which underlie the social and ethical relations of men and that failure to observe them affects always the personal self by disturbing the stream of consciousness. As we have seen, this self is no more than the thought and feeling of the day, the hour, the moment, associated with a sum representing the thoughts and feelings of the past. Harmony is the condition to be preserved, for where we are out of harmony with others, we are thrown out of harmony within ourselves. If we are not just and kind in our relations and in our thoughts of men, the character of the self must suffer. It is impossible to injure others without injuring self, and whatever benefit we confer upon others we at the same time confer upon ourselves.

Thought is antecedent to act. All relations are then fundamentally in thought and the supervision and control of consciousness is the first necessity. Whatever may exist outside of my own mind, one thing is certain, I can perceive it only through my mind, and what I know is never the thing itself but my concept of it. Now a disturbed mind is more likely to arrive at false than at true concepts. Unfortunately the mind reacts upon false ideas quite as readily as upon true, and it is just such reactions as this which cause most of our troubles both mental and physical.

This fact received the greatest emphasis from that most pregnant discovery of psychology, namely that *all consciousness is motor*, that is, all feelings, no matter how slight, necessarily produce movement of some sort, through the nerve centres, but not in the voluntary muscles alone, for it may expend itself on the viscera. In this connection, Professor Bain says:

> According as an impression is accompanied with feeling, the aroused currents diffuse themselves over the brain, leading to a general agitation of the moving organs, as well as affecting the viscera.

Professor James has this to say:

> We have now experimental proof that the heart-beats, the arterial pressure, the respiration, the sweat-glands, the pupil, the bladder, bowels, and uterus, as well as the voluntary muscles, may have their tone and degree of contraction altered even by the most insignificant sensorial stimuli.

The foregoing is sufficient intimation for the present moment of that relation of mind and body which we shall consider in Part II. Let it be remembered in this connection that all sensation is necessarily in consciousness. If we are not conscious of it there is no sensation. Activity there may be of some sort, but sensation there is not. Pain and pleasure are in the mind, are mental states within the stream of consciousness. Just so, sight and hearing are purely the results of acts of consciousness. The eye itself can no more see than a telescope can see; the ear is as incapable of hearing as a telephone receiver. It is perfectly true that out of consciousness there is neither light nor sound, but vibration merely, which through the instruments of eye and ear induces in the recipient mind those sensations we know as light and sound.

Consciousness must necessarily have an object. If that object be the body, if it be wholly engrossed with the material self, it is very likely to produce bodily disorder and certainly it is an unprofitable state of mind; for it is Spirit which quickeneth and flesh profits little or nothing beyond being an efficient instrument of the mind's activities. Too much attention to the body invariably produces trouble. While it should have reasonable care, if pampered it readily induces a false consciousness and the material self becomes a tyrant usurping the place of true and better selves.

We choose our objects of consciousness; that is, we elect that plane upon which we shall dwell in thought. A sane mind will tend to distribute its energy, ignoring no plane but giving most attention where it is most worth while. As long as we have bodies we cannot live as though we had them not, but it may be laid down as a good rule that the less thought centred on the body, the better. Where were we intended to dwell in thought? Certainly not like animals concerned only with eating and reproduction. We are fitted normally for an intellectual and spiritual life. Yet you will see plenty of silly people whose main object in life is to get fat, or to get thin, and who have little interest in anything besides their bodies. We must rise, as far as expedient, above a purely material consciousness and acquire the habit of dwelling upon higher planes of thought; starve out false ideas by giving them no attention, while we cultivate the true and beautiful. First is the natural man and then the spiritual. There is always an evolution going on in the normal mind, a slow spiritualisation of the faculties, a tendency towards truth and away from error.

"As a man thinketh in his heart, so is he," or, more properly, so is the self as known. The Soul—always the self as knower—must of necessity remain unchanged, notwithstanding the mutations of the personal self. Let consciousness, then, be centred upon Truth as its normal object of perception, that it may more and more bring the truth into manifestation, and a sickly or unprofitable self-consciousness be replaced by a sane and wholesome God-consciousness; that the true self—the free and perfect Soul—may be reflected in mind.

CHAPTER V

RELIGION

LET us come directly at the essence of Religion, which is man's relation to God—as Ethics is his relation to man—putting aside that class of ideas which has to do with the form of religion as foreign to our purpose. There is no possible objection to the ceremonial, in so far as it is beautiful, but unless we have at the same time the realisation of the presence of God within us, the rest counts for little. The point to be made is that, whereas ethics and morals are essential, ceremonial may be beautiful, good music inspiring, and the social life of a church agreeable, these things are not religion nor are they adequate substitutes for it.

Religion with Jesus himself was not a question of creeds and dogmas at all; it was simply the attainment of God-consciousness, the *realisation* of God within oneself. This is the true inwardness of religion and it has ever been the religious ideal in the East. Now we have borrowed our religion from the East—we have none of our own—and therefore in all justice to Jesus whom we regard as the founder of that religion, and in all justice to the true idea of religion, let us borrow correctly and not garble and misconstrue the teaching of a man who saw truth as perhaps no other ever has, the most spiritually awakened man the world has known. The spirit of these remarks is not to be construed as antagonistic to true Christian ideals, but rather as a plea for a right interpretation of the religion of Jesus—a true conception of religion itself.

We are here concerned, not with morals, but with religion, notwithstanding morality is so essential to a religious life,—is the concomitant of any true and sane life. But mark you, a system of morals is not religion. The relation of morality to religion was expressed in the saying, "The light of the body is the eye: if, therefore, thine eye be single, thy whole body shall be full of light. But if thine eye be evil, thy whole body shall be full of darkness. If, therefore, the light that is in thee be darkness, how great is that darkness." In other words, a moral defect may vitiate the whole stream of consciousness. Immorality implies impurity, selfishness, and insincerity, all of which are veils which prevent the mind from perceiving Truth.

With Jesus religion was practical; it was not a matter of form, for that was precisely what he so disparaged in the Scribes and Pharisees of his time; neither was it for set times and places—not for Sundays but for all days. He lived by it, in short. He aimed constantly to bring God into consciousness. If we are to associate him with any doctrine, it is the glorious truth of the liberty of the Soul. That for which he stood, above all, was the triumph of spirit over the flesh.

Here we have the essence of this great man's teaching, which was just that identity of the self as knower with God, the Supreme Knower of the Universe. Ask yourself then, you who profess the religion of Jesus, how much does your religion mean to you the liberty of the Soul, the triumph of spirit over matter, the identity of the real man in you with God? How far have you brought God into consciousness by thinking good and thinking love and by giving room only to these in your thoughts? Whatever else religion may be, it is fundamentally a matter of *real-*

isation, and only the truth we have *realised* avails us at all. Is our thirst quenched by reading about water or repeating prayers to Neptune? Are we warmed by singing hymns to Apollo? Yet much of our religion amounts to no more than this. We derive no help from it for there is no help in it.

Religion is an affair of one's self and God. But the Soul is God in us; hence we may say that religion is Soul-realisation or Self-knowledge. It should be the most vital and practical relation in life. Man is a stream of which God is the Source. In his religious life he shall keep the stream open to that immortal spring from which it comes and without which it would be nothing. We have our life in God and life other than this there is none. Only in consciousness are we separated from God, and the one vital thing in religion is to bring ourselves into a conscious relationship and to make that permanent. We have wisdom and strength in proportion as this is accomplished in us; we are weak and foolish so long as it is not. For God is the only source of love and truth, of health and strength.

Conventionally we assume to approach God in our prayers, and these prayers are, for the most part, mere petitions for something already latent in us which we have not brought into manifestation. All petitions to an extra-cosmic God for a change in the established order of things are as vain as they are childish. Rather should we aim in our prayers to get in harmony with that order.

What then is true prayer? It is a lifting up of the heart to better things, if you wish, and this is time well spent. Prayer in this sense is practically auto-suggestion, and whenever thought is centred upon true and uplifting ideals, it cannot fail to be an efficient force in regeneration. It works either way, however, and if we dwell upon false concepts we get a negative reaction quite as readily as we experience a positive one when we dwell upon true ideals. But more than this, prayer —if it means anything—is the effort to bring into realisation our own identity with God, and in this the lips have no part. It is to be accomplished in silence by the exclusion of all ideas of the world and of the personal self, and persistent meditation and concentration upon the reality of Being and fundamental Truth itself. We have seen that through consciousness we cannot know God, inasmuch as God is the subject, never the object of knowledge, and all we can ever attain to, in the nature of things, by that process will still be only our own consciousness of God. Eastern thinkers, however, have always maintained that, while God cannot directly be known through consciousness, he can be known through super-consciousness, that state in which the idea of the personal self with its limitations is transcended completely and the sense of separateness incidental to it is replaced by the spiritual sense of union with God. However that may be, the idea has sufficient ground in philosophy to make the effort worth while, for it is surely a strengthening and spiritualising process.

But whenever we dwell upon the good, the true, and the beautiful we are drawing nearer to God, and all conscious effort in that direction is prayer. Whatever we hold in mind we tend to bring into externalisation. Hence it is that thoughts of weakness, of poverty, of sickness, of malice are also prayers—unwise prayers which work us harm. Let us have a care, then, that we pray wisely. We have already prayed ourselves into much trouble, and by reversing the order and dwelling upon Truth instead of error, we can pray ourselves out again.

The attitude that Jesus assumed to the

world and the worldly life, while doubtless extreme, was sufficiently grounded in wisdom and in a sound philosophy of life to commend itself to us. The Kingdom of Heaven, he affirmed, is within; not meat and drink, but righteousness and peace. In other words, it is no more than a state of mind in harmony with Truth and Love—a God-consciousness. "Except a man be born again, he cannot see the Kingdom of God"; again, "That which is born of the flesh is flesh; and that which is born of the Spirit is spirit." The worldly mind and the spiritual mind are not in harmony. One is selfishness and unrest, the other, love and peace; one is subjection to illusion, the other the perception of Truth. Hence it is impossible to follow both and every man must choose for himself which he shall serve, whether God or Mammon, whether he shall seek Truth or pursue the phantom world, whether live from within or from without. The admonition to lay not up where moth and rust corrupt and to labour not for the perishable, but for that which endures, is in line with this point of view and absolutely sound in principle, though it may easily be exaggerated in application. Where the treasure is there will the heart be. A mind devoted to pleasure or to money-getting has no leisure, and eventually no inclination, for the consideration of more profitable things. The harm is not in money, but the love of money to the exclusion of all else; not in the world itself, but in the deadening of the spiritual life in us by the acceptance of false and worldly ideals; not in the body, which is good in itself, but in the slavery to the senses, the degradation of the mind which is the natural result of living to the body. These false ways of living and thinking pollute the stream of consciousness; therefore, and for this good and sufficient reason,—"Be not conformed to this world, but be ye transformed by the renewing of your minds."

To live to the body is a living death, for there is no greater tyrant than a pampered body. To live to the world is to invite despair, for there is no happiness in the worldly life. Only as we live by the Spirit shall we have peace and the joy of the inner life; only as we live from within, shall we have any measure of freedom.

CHAPTER VI

ETHICS 

BEFORE concluding this brief survey of First Principles, let us for a moment glance at ethical relations. For it may be laid down as a basic fact that we can have no relation with any other self which does not affect the nature of our own self. Whatever we think of others necessarily induces in us a certain state of mind, and if our relation be selfish or uncharitable we perforce mar our own minds by our perverted view. If on the other hand it be kind and unselfish, we purify and elevate the content of our minds accordingly.

Consciousness is not absolutely our own; it is localised in us and receives a particular stamp as it were, but it is connected always with the race consciousness, as the water in a bay, an estuary, or a strait is one with the water in the sea, though partly confined and given a definite form by the shore line. When it is high tide in the sea, it is high tide in the bay as well. Thus in a measure we are always open to and influenced by the world-thought, the mental atmosphere in which we live. Never are we wholly independent of it. A change in that atmosphere is liable to affect us, be it little or much, according to the kind of influence to which we are peculiarly susceptible. Epidemics, panics, contagions, fads, and fashions exert their power largely through this; by its means any wave sent out may reach to numbers of individual minds, as a tidal wave having its origin at sea may affect all the bays along the shore.

While we are subject to the thought of the whole world, we are of course more directly influenced by people in our own town or our own circle; and when it comes to our own family and friends our feelings are so interwoven with theirs that we are influenced telepathically by their moods and thoughts. We are never completely isolated units; there is no such thing as an absolutely solitary person. Harmony is the basis of a happy life,—a completely sane life. Whether we consider philosophy, religion, or ethics,—in one and all, harmony is the end in view; in philosophy it is harmony within oneself, in religion harmony with God, and in ethics a harmonious relationship with one's fellow-men. For that matter health is harmony. We may be said, with some show of reason, to have a race-self, a national-self, and a family-self all of which are merely expansions of the ego or social self. Whatever affects these must influence us somewhere on the confines of consciousness,—the border of the stream if not in its main currents.

Now the harmony of a family is of course dependent upon the attitude of the several units which compose that body. Perhaps it will suffice for our present purpose if we emphasise the psychic nature of the peculiarly subtle relations which make up social and, in particular, family life. The subject receives added importance when we remember that what affects any one member must of necessity affect the family as a whole; as a disturbance in the eye lessens the comfort of the entire body. There is, therefore, nothing more necessary in life than to do one's share towards establishing and maintaining harmony in our relations with others—and charity begins at home. The basis of true relationship is love and considerateness; the arch enemy of the home—of society in fact—is selfishness arising from ignorance. For could we realise that, by inexorable laws, every injury we do to another, we do to some part of ourselves as well; that every injustice is at the same time a self-deprivation; that the quality of thought we send out to others comes back to us,—could we grow wise, in other words—the world would wear a different face and life would be sweetened. But as a fact the world wears just such a face as we give it. To the cheerful it is bright and to the crabbed, sour. If we have love in our hearts we attract love We radiate those qualities which are ascendant in us. Whether we speak or not, our thought is going from us continuously and others are receiving those thoughts like wireless messages.

In the attempt to establish harmony, it is evident we must begin with ourselves. For my own attitude of mind is an incentive or a stumbling-block to everyone I meet. They may rise superior to its unrest or they may fail to respond to its serenity; in either case it is provocative of one condition or another and the stronger mind, or the stronger mood, will dominate. It is no more than reasonable that we should endeavour to preserve tranquillity in our own minds, not alone for our immediate benefit but for the effect it must have upon others; and to do this we shall have to withstand and repel the untoward thoughts of others as well as to guard our own.

If you live in an atmosphere of inharmony, your mind is functioning under unfavorable conditions, precisely as the lungs perform their work at a disadvantage in impure air. We normally require a psychic atmosphere of love and harmony, as we need a physical atmosphere of fresh air. Every one has something which stands to him as home, his own particular and familiar mental environment, as every one lives in a house or shelter of some sort, and in that home he spends a good part of his time and its atmosphere is more personal to him than is any other. Therefore we shall strike at the root of what we have to say on the relation of ethics to our subject if we address ourselves to a consideration of the home. If in your house the windows are kept closed and the air is heavy and impure you cannot constantly breathe such air without ultimately feeling its debilitating effect. But if in your home the mental atmosphere is stale and heavy, or electric and discordant, its effect upon the mind and thence upon the body is far more potent still. Now home, like heaven, is a state of love and harmony, and alas! there are many homeless families in the world; people who are well housed, but who never know that state wherein unselfishness, considerateness, forbearance, geniality and tact prevail. These homeless ones are slowly starved for lack of spiritual nourishment, or gradually poisoned by the mental atmosphere in which they live. For while we may withstand inharmony for a short time, we cannot live in it without having the whole mental life infected; unless indeed we are able to exert a tremendous force of love and wisdom in self-protection. Rest assured we can no more do without sunshine in our hearts than without sunshine in our houses. When we have not a home in the true sense of the word, the very springs of social life are touched. Before we lay our troubles to the climate, the coffee, or the cooking, let us examine ourselves whether we have a home or not, and first as to whether we are doing our share to that end. Wherever our emotions enter, the effect on mental conditions is far stronger. Hence, as feeling enters into our life in the home more than in other social relations, the mental reactions are more acute because more personal.

While we have seen to it that the house is clean, the sanitary conditions good, the ventilation as it should be, let us survey the condition of the home from time to time with equal care. First, does it rest on sincerity? For insincerity is a dry rot which will undermine any foundation. Love and sincerity must be the basis of any true relation and it were better to have no relations with people whatever than to have insincere ones. Every insincerity we harbor weakens the mental and moral fibre and will make itself known by inviting negative conditions. In this, every man is his own friend or his own foe.

Without love and sincerity there cannot possibly be harmony, and a discordant home is a house divided against itself, a castle which will be taken by every onslaught of negative conditions from without. But a true home is a fortress of strength, wherein the several members are mentally and morally invigorated in the atmosphere of harmony and love to cope with the ignorance and selfishness of the world. We must realise that harmony is dependent upon psychic conditions more often felt than known and often too subtle for analysis. But if we are being mentally or morally poisoned in the home, the day's work, the whole life, must suffer. It goes without saying that it is much easier to discover and correct our own defects if we will but cease focusing our thoughts on the defects of others. Let us once do this and look ourselves in the face and we shall see that we countenance a number of minor faults which, nevertheless, cause friction and militate against that harmony which it is our own best interest to preserve; tactlessness, for instance, inconsiderateness in little things, foibles and whims, prejudices, vanity, irritability—these are the microbes in the household which ever and anon lay us low. The critical habit, again, is fatal to harmonious relations. Let us agree to mind our own business and never to criticise except in love and with the view of helping others to help themselves—simply because it is the best way to do. Common sense and spiritual prudence alike demand it.

All of this might have been said in high-sounding phrases, but we are here concerned with facts, not theories, and it is just these commonplaces of life which reveal whether we have any ethics worthy the name. The home life is an expression of the personal self,—is a larger self, which is peculiarly susceptible to the relation to others, but which at the same time affects every other phase of the personal self. If we could establish the home on love, sincerity, and truth, social conditions would take care of themselves. We cannot like everybody; we cannot find every one congenial. Social lines are not as arbitrary as they seem, for people are drawn together or repelled by subtle affinities and repulsions, and naturally segregate according to degrees of breeding and culture and community in taste and opinions. But we can do good; we can bless, we can think no evil, and it is with this that Ethics is concerned. Love and service are normal to life. We have no true life without them. Selfishness and malice are abnormal and can be removed, as weeds can be uprooted in a garden in order that the flowers themselves may thrive and bloom.

Modern thought has brought to light the importance of our psychic relations and emphasised the fact that it is not only what we do unto others, but what we *think* of others that counts. For as you think of others, such in part is the content of your own mind, that glass through which you look; and as that glass is clear or opaque, in focus or out of focus, so will the world appear to you, and so life itself. Now harmony above all things tends to keep the glass in focus.

PART II

PRACTICAL PSYCHOLOGY

PRACTICAL PSYCHOLOGY

IN this outline of practical psychology the idea which has inspired the book, namely self-help through utilising our own forces, will be emphasised throughout. "The great thing, then, in all education," says William James, "is to make our nervous system our ally instead of our enemy." Now, that is the key-note of a psychology that is to be of any use to us, or to have any interest outside of the lecture-room.

The force and value of practical psychology lies in making allies of our faculties, in making friends instead of enemies, in establishing true and wise relations in place of antagonism with nature and with whatever is good in the world-thought as well. Not only the nervous system but the will, the emotions, the imagination, the energy of thought and the force of habit should one and all serve us, should be our good allies working for us and not against us. As the floods and the lightning work us harm, thus are our own forces inimical to us when uncontrolled or misdirected. But of more value to us than running streams or electric currents is our thought-energy when properly directed and fully utilised.

We have it in our power to establish this general harmony within ourselves, allowing no force to go to waste and none to work harm, but bringing all into line that they may function to the best advantage, while we derive the good from each and all. Our religion should help us to appropriate the divine energy in our spiritual life, as we appropriate the energy of the sun in our physical life. Our applied psychology must help us to direct and utilise the stream of consciousness so that it shall run our thought-mill to good purpose. It will teach us to form good habits in place of bad, to think positive and healthy thoughts instead of sick and negative ones, to be our own friend instead of our own enemy, by bringing the real man into consciousness.

CHAPTER I

THOUGHT AND THE BRAIN

SO much has been said of late on the subject of thought-control and the relation of the mind to the body, that the idea has unfortunately become rather hackneyed—unfortunately, for the simple reason that our minds are so readily blunted by the habitual or familiar, that when a truth becomes a truism it no longer makes any impression. While there is not much left to be said on this subject that has not already been said, we may be pardoned for referring to some of its practical aspects.

The stream of consciousness uses the brain as its instrument and has been clearly shown to model that organ more or less according to the nature and extent of its activity. Professor Gates in experimenting with guinea-pigs by training one animal in a certain direction and not the other, has found on examining the brains of the two animals, that the one whose faculties had thus been encouraged showed an enormous development in the corresponding brain area over the one which had not so been treated. In other words, stimulating the mind had rapidly promoted cellular growth in the brain.

We have every reason to infer that in this manner all areas of the brain may be developed by persistent thought through channels which use these particular areas. Thus an artist, a linguist, a mathematician, each tends by the exercise of his profession to develop certain areas above others. A thoroughly well cultivated mind must tend to increase all brain-areas more or less; a well balanced mind will cultivate no one at the expense of others; while an unbalanced person has either cultivated one area out of all proportion to the rest, or failed wholly with regard to some which are essential to normal thinking. The fact is, we develop our brains through thinking, very much as we perfect our muscular system through exercise.

Doubtless the most important discovery of psycho-physiology is the fact that, whereas the sense areas of the brain are congenital, the "thinking" areas are acquired. Huxley has shown that the brains of an infant and of a chimpanzee are practically identical. Man, however, proceeds from infancy to create centres in his brain by his social, intellectual and emotional life, while the brain of the ape remains unchanged. Man then, does not receive these centres ready-made, but creates them through the quality and direction of his thought. He may inherit a talent, but he does not inherit the brain to go with it; for this he must mould to suit his purpose, as a potter fashions the clay. We have long known that faculties grow through use, but only recently has it been understood that by their use we were actually fashioning a brain to further that expression, as a gymnast develops a body to suit his particular needs.

The brain is a paired organ; that is to say, we really have two brains, and it is a curious fact that these "thinking" areas, including the speech centre, are developed in one brain only, normally in the left hemisphere. Around the centres of sight and hearing with which we were born, we create and develop others—a reading centre, for instance, and a music centre. Now if an injury to the brain should destroy the music centre while leaving the centre of hearing intact, as has been known to happen, we still might *hear* our best-beloved airs, but without being able to understand or enjoy them. As the acquired centres have been created in only one hemisphere—usually the left—if the right brain be destroyed and the left remain unimpaired, we may still read and enjoy music as before, and a case of this kind has occurred. If on the other hand a particular centre is injured in the left brain—or speaking brain as it is known—that centre may possibly be developed in the right hemisphere. If the reading centre, for instance, be destroyed, the patient must learn to read over again, precisely as he did when a child, and little by little create in his right hemisphere another reading centre.

Such are some of the facts adduced after long and patient investigation in a difficult field by students of the brain. Dr. Thompson compares an acquired centre to a shelf upon which, in the process of development, we place book after book. In view of these facts, the materialistic assumption that the brain secretes thought, as the liver secretes bile, is more absurd than ever. The mind builds the brain by the extent and quality of its activity. This is done largely in the plastic years. In youth we elect what sort of a brain we shall have for use in subsequent years. Early interest in music, literature, and art fashions a brain which will react more readily under stimuli of that nature throughout life. Early habits of right-thinking establish neural paths through which thought will tend to flow ever after. But we are always modifying our brains by the character of our thought. It is more difficult in middle life than in youth, simply because we tend to react along paths already established in the brain, as we incline to follow beaten paths in the woods. This difficulty has doubtless been exaggerated. With systematic auto-suggestion and the larger comprehension of the mental action which is now possible, we may accomplish much that has heretofore seemed impossible. In fact where shall we draw the line? No one knows what he can do until he has tried, and each success, each victory, and every addition of knowledge, fits us for a greater victory.

The practical bearing of the foregoing remarks must be obvious to the reader, and it will be doubly so when we come to consider the nervous system in relation to thought. We are creating our brains, just as if we were to fashion a violin upon which to play, and unless we have made a good instrument we cannot hope to give a very good performance in life. The gist of the matter is that we—the personal self, that is—fashion the instrument, we keep it in tune or out of tune, we make of it a first-class instrument or a poor one, and meanwhile we have to saw away on it the best we can. If the result is sometimes hard on our friends, let us in all decency improve matters, for we have it within our power to do so.

We need, however, give little further heed to the instrument, but concern ourselves rather with that force which fashions the instrument, namely Thought. The fact to be borne in mind with reference to the brain is that it always tends to react along established paths, and therefore by wrong habits of thought we make it increasingly difficult for ourselves to think clearly. Beliefs and prejudices long entertained have lent their impressions to the brain; therefore the sooner we begin to eliminate them, the better.

In comparing the brain to an instrument we must, however, remember that the player works from within. Harmony of mind tends to produce a normal and harmonious instrument. It is for us to keep ourselves in harmony, then, and the brain will take care of itself. To do this, however, involves the various relations of life, and none more than the ethical relations. In the next chapter we shall see how the mental states affect the body through the nervous system. For the present, let us consider merely the influence of the quality of thought upon the mind itself, remembering that it is the persistent habits of thought which model the brain. Consciousness, as we have seen, is a flowing stream. The mind constantly generates thought-energy. Much of this energy goes to waste. Much is misdirected and works harm. Looked at in this light, the propriety of harnessing and directing that thought-energy at once appeals to our common sense. This is the first step in self-help. Your mind is your own; you are liberating this energy, and yet you have been wasting and misdirecting it for years to your own harm. Now you are to take control and make this energy serve your purpose.

It has been the same with the forces of Nature. How long did electrical energy, gravity, and water-power go unharnessed! Yet now they serve us admirably. We were not able to utilise them, however, until we not only had discovered the fundamental laws of motion, of hydraulics, of mechanics, and so on, but their application as well, and this came much later. Similarly, in psychology it has long been known that consciousness is motor in its effect, but it is only recently that we have fully realised the practical bearing of this important fact and begun to apply it in Suggestion. This is a practical age, and while Poetry and Art suffer because of this modern utilitarianism, the Sciences have gained by it; and none more than psychology, for psychology is of little use unless it is practical.

As a machine must be devised with reference to the laws of motion and of mechanics if it is to utilise the energy supplied to it, so must we devise and control our thought-energy with reference to fundamental laws of Thought if we are to use that energy to advantage If a machine is not properly constructed or placed, not only will it not do its work, but it will throw itself out of gear. Now this is just what happens with a wrongly directed mind; it does poor work and throws the nervous system out of order. There is a normal way of thinking, a normal attitude towards the different relations of life, which we have briefly reviewed in Part I. In regard to some of these we are wofully ignorant; in others we *know* much better than we *do*, but in either case we always experience the result of wrong thinking whether we knew better or did not. If you handle your automobile ignorantly or carelessly you may break the machine or you may yourself be injured; what you suffer is not a penalty, but merely the result of your act. It may serve to teach, however, the proper way to manage the machine.

We know fairly well what our attitude to one another should be and on the whole we endeavour to maintain it—outside of war and business—for man inclines more naturally to kindness than the reverse. We fail to realise how subtle that relation is, however; that our thoughts of people count for or against our peace of mind as well. We may fool other people, but we do not so often deceive ourselves and we never deceive our brains. We may pretend to anything we wish, but all the time our real motives are moulding our brains and establishing neural paths quite at variance with our pretensions. The normal attitude to our fellow-men is love, kindness, and forbearance—forbearance, because if we understood the conditions which have made them what they are we should no longer be inclined to judge. All we can hope to do is to maintain our own minds in harmony with this fact and to radiate this quality of thought. If we cannot get on with some people we can let them alone, but in any case we must still aim to keep in harmony with the normal relation. What others do is their concern. If they fail they must get the results of their mistakes. But in so far as we preserve the integrity of our own minds and hearts, we help others to do the same, for love and good-will are contagious. The quality of thought we send out to people is very apt to be returned to us, considerateness for considerateness, antagonism for antagonism. We are social beings, and of all our relations in life the social is uppermost in consciousness and is more involved with the emotions. Hence the states of mind which it induces are more active in influence for good or harm. Love is the great norm of human life, and wherever consciousness is at variance with this it is temporarily abnormal. It is as fundamental to a balanced mind as the laws of motion to a machine. Our thinking, our living, amounts to little in the end if we have not love in our hearts.

Similarly we may say there is a normal attitude towards God and towards life itself, and the philosophy of life is to discover and maintain this in consciousness. For whenever we fail to do so, the mental reactions are discordant and, persisted in, develop some kinks in the brain which make it easy to react that way in future. The normal attitude to God is love and trust, and, more than this, the effort to realise God within ourselves. For, as we have seen, the self as knower—the Soul—being in fact God within us, we are separated from Him only in consciousness, and it is in consciousness we must bridge that apparent gulf and replace that sense of separateness with an overwhelming realisation of the immanence of God—God the Absolute Love and Truth, whose energy we should normally appropriate in our lives. This, at the same time, amounts to bringing the real and unchangeable man into expression.

Towards nature, the normal attitude is by all means a friendly one, for, as we shall see when we come to consider the subject of Belief, the attitude towards any object reacts upon us, though the idea in mind be entirely false. Make friends in nature, then; make friends of mankind, a friend of God. Go with the current by assuming the normal attitude toward all things. Make friends of the air and water, of heat and cold, of food and drink, for you do not fear your friend. Every fear in your mind works you harm, but your friends rally to your support; love works for you always.

First and last be your own friend, for if you have not harmony within you are a house divided against itself. Consider well the nature of the personal self—that multitude of ephemeral and shadowy persons whom we galvanise into apparent life by the energy of thought, only to let them fade away into nothingness—and learn to distinguish it from the true self, the wise and unfettered Soul which is God within you, unchanging and unchangeable. Deathless, diseaseless, ageless, untroubled in a world of sorrow—it is to the Soul you shall turn as to your refuge and your strength, to that you shall cling as to the Rock of Ages. It is merely a habit that we identify ourselves always with the flowing stream of consciousness. Let us now substitute the habit of identifying ourselves with that alone which is not subject to fear—the immortal Soul.

Aim to preserve your mental states always

in harmony with this inner model of love, wisdom, and strength. Let all your concepts be in line with it, and whatever is alien to it exclude from your consciousness. Post, as it were, a guard at the door of the mind and examine every thought which applies for admittance, whether it be in accord with the good government of the mind or antagonistic to it, in which case eject it summarily. In good time, if this vigorous inspection be established, these anarchists of the mind will no longer apply for admission. But once you let them in, they will by their very nature make trouble till you get them out again.

Every thought of fear, or of selfishness—in any one of their many guises—separates us that much in consciousness from God, the absolute Truth, and by each separation we are weakened, for God is the one Source of life and strength. But every true concept, every thought of love, draws us nearer to God by bringing love and truth into consciousness and thus strengthens and fortifies us.

The Science of the Mind, reduced to its simplest terms, is the perception of normal attitudes in the several relations of life and the practice of right-thinking, that normal reactions in mind and body shall be encouraged and unfavourable reactions be inhibited. The necessity for this will more fully appear when we turn our attention to the relation of thought to the nervous system.

CHAPTER II

THOUGHT AND THE NERVOUS SYSTEM

THE nervous system is but the extension of brain material to a distance from the main centres, or more correctly, the brain is but the culmination of the nervous system. For in the course of evolution there were nervous systems long before there were brains. The spinal cord with its various centres is a sort of brain—an automatic brain, acting like a switch-board—but not a thinking brain. From these centres or sub-stations, nerves radiate to the several organs, automatically enabling them to function. With the lower orders of animals such an arrangement is all they need for their uncomplicated existence with its simple reactions, for their acts are all reflexive or automatic. A nervous system is sufficient for a wholly automatic existence. As they ascend the scale the brain gradually develops, playing at first but a small part in the nervous economy of the animal.

In man the nervous system takes much the same part that it does in the lower animal, but in place of being wholly automatic it is under the supervision of a thinking brain and—as we shall presently see—whether this is an advantage or a disadvantage depends largely upon the kind of thinking that is done. A spinal centre left to itself automatically works the organs under its control. But from the brain come nerves to each centre which carry messages from head-quarters, relevant or irrelevant to the nature of that particular centre's activities. Thus the nerves whose office is to operate the heart, we will say, have nothing to do with things outside of their own sphere. Nerves from the thinking brain, however, bring a current to that centre, the result of some thought process wholly foreign to the heart or its action, and the condition of the heart is at once influenced by the effect of that message upon the motor centre. We are therefore less concerned here with these automatic centres than with the nerves which convey currents induced by thoughts and feelings through the brain, and we shall confine our attention principally to those thoughts and feelings themselves. For nerves are merely the wires which convey messages or which open and close switches.

As far as the physical man is concerned, however, we may regard him as merely a nervous system, for no muscle or organ operates itself, but all are operated by the controlling nerves. Whatever influences the action of the nerve, then, must affect the organ. Now this is just what happens with all organs, though it is obvious only in particular instances. Fright, for example, is an emotion which sends a peculiar current to the heart centre, preventing the automatic nerves from working in the normal way, and thus either retarding or accelerating the action of that organ. In this manner the heart's action may be stopped entirely and this in all probability has not infrequently happened.

Nerves which ramify throughout the arteries, contract or enlarge these vessels and, while perhaps originally wholly automatic in their action, they are now, at any rate, interfered with by every passing emotion, so that the mere sight of a spider on the coat-sleeve will in some persons affect the distribution of the circulation. Self-consciousness, anger, fear become evident in changing the pressure of blood to the face. To produce a flush or a pallor, however, they must first have influenced the action of the viscera. That is, a thought has this motor consequence and the nerves are the means which have made such a result possible, we may say inevitable.

It has been found that by placing the arm in a vessel of water full to the brim and then concentrating the thought upon that member, the circulation would so increase that the arm would swell, which was at once indicated by the water overflowing. Professor Gates has ascertained by experiment that, by applying suitable reagents to the blood, a reaction was obtained from the blood taken from a person in anger different from the reaction when the blood was taken from one in some other mood. In fact an acid of a poisonous character had been produced by the state of anger. Under similar conditions the breath has been analysed and found to vary with the emotions. There is reason to suppose that the secretions and the perspiration are similarly affected. From so pertinent a fact we can hardly fail to draw the obvious deductions. It serves as much as any fact can to emphasise the exceedingly intimate nature of that relation which obtains between thought and the nervous system; that is, the relation of mind and body. The bladder, the bowels, and the stomach are apparently as sensitive as the heart to nervous reactions through thought stimulus.

It is evident that if a temporary mood, as of anger or of fear, produces a nervous reaction and a temporary physical change, a persistent mood—an habitual state of irritability or fear—must perpetuate this in the body until that class of nervous reactions becomes usual and a changed action of the viscera and a different condition of the blood are the result. As all consciousness is motor, every state of mind must outwardly picture itself in the body. In fact, as we have seen in considering First Principles, the body has no life apart from the mind; it is the visible and material effect of an invisible and mental cause, and all its activities vary from moment to moment as the nervous reactions are affected by the fluctuations in the thought current.

While organic functions are thus responsive to neural conditions, the nervous system itself, unlike telephone wires, must be somewhat affected by the quality of the currents which pass through it. Nerves wear out, so to speak, by being overused by currents of fear or excitability, as does a piano wire by the constant hammering on a particular note. In the general excitement of this age and the intensity of life, the nerves of a whole people are constantly keyed up, and the result is the prevalence of nervous disorders and the almost universal tendency to nervous depletion. The common state of mind to-day is one of over-stimulation and consequent depression. The remedy is repose, relaxation, recreation, instead of which the tendency is to further excite and stimulate. As far as we are physically concerned nothing can be more essential than a sound nervous system, which is far more to be desired than muscular development. Mental strain and excitement, insufficient repose, and immoderate use of stimulants all conspire to deprive us of this.

But the chief enemy of the nervous system is misdirected or uncontrolled thought. The association between a mental state and a nervous reaction is so close that they may be considered as practically one, like water and ice or vapour and cloud. "All mental states (no matter what their character as regards utility may be)," says Professor James, "are followed by bodily activity of some sort. They lead to inconspicuous changes in breathing, circulation, general muscular tension, and glandular or other visceral activity, even if they do not lead to conspicuous movements of the muscles of voluntary life. Not only certain particular states of mind, then (such as those called volitions, for example), but states of mind as such, *all* states of mind, even mere thoughts and feelings, are *motor* in their consequences." We may set it down as one of the fundamental facts of psychology that wherever the normal attitude in any of the relations of life is not maintained, the attendant nervous reaction will disturb the health of the body and of the nervous system itself.

To be "nervous" is to fail in some essential of self-control. But it must be granted that the condition of the body reacts upon the mind, just as truly as the state of mind influences the body. Let this fact, however, be understood, not *mis*understood, as are so many facts wherever they seem to prove something which we want to have true. Thus it were more accurate to say in this connection that the mind, taking cognizance of a bodily condition, reacts upon itself. And this it does not only with reference to our bodies, but our clothes as well. If I feel nervous because you drum with your feet, it is not your drumming which really fusses me, but my feeling about your drumming. While the drumming is the occasion, it is my dislike of drumming which causes my irritable state, and it is this irritable state which translates itself into nervousness. This is a very small matter in itself, yet if I foster rather than overcome a sensitiveness to drumming and a hundred other trifles of this nature, the result is increased susceptibility—nervousness, that is,—until neural paths are formed and the nervous mechanism reacts apparently without any intervening consciousness of dislike.

One may not be able to stop the drumming, and even so would still remain susceptible to every other annoyance; but if by self-control we overcome susceptibility, the cause is banished which gave rise to the unpleasant reactions. Though the occasion should still persist it no longer produces a reaction. Here we have the cause and the cure for incipient nervous disorder. Allowed to become habitual, however, the chronic *dis*ease of mind records itself in chronic *dis*ease of the nerves; for, as we have seen, a mental state and its nervous reaction are practically one and the same.

Let a discordant mental state produce some bodily disorder and this reacts again upon the consciousness of self to further depress the mind. The body, inert in itself, thus exerts a power of suggestion over the mind. It were foolish to ignore this fact, for any inanimate object may do this. Thus the sight of food or of a bottle may suggest to us the act of eating and drinking and we may at once feel hungry and thirsty though we had not thought of this a moment before. A cigar suggests that we smoke, a stream that we fish or bathe, a book that we read. It must be remembered, however, that these objects do not act of themselves, but are merely the occasions of the reaction in the mind of the beholder. It is the perception, or properly the apperception, of the object which through suggestion induces a particular state of mind.

While mind and body may thus be said to react upon each other, sensation no less than feeling is purely a mental state. The body cannot feel, but it induces sensation in the mind. As far as this life is concerned, mind and body are inseparable. The one important truth in this connection to which the New Thought movement, and for that matter any spiritual philosophy, is committed, is that the mind, not the body, feels and acts, and the mind should rule the body rather than the body the mind. To be a slave to sensation is to be in bondage to those states of mind which the body induces by suggestion, and this means the same thing as bondage to the body itself—a degradation of consciousness from which the New Thought is but one of those many spiritual reactions which have taken place in the history of philosophy.

That the mind should rule the body by making sensation subject to reason and will, is the normal attitude. But as far as the direct relation of mind and body is concerned, wisdom lies in taking the mind off the body as far as expedient. The less thought is centred on the body, the more freedom have the automatic centres to do their work in accordance with that universal mind we call Nature. Our little minds obstruct and interfere and the result is apt to be discordant nervous reactions. Keep the mind pure, free, and tranquil, let it be dominated by love and truth, and the body will apparently take care of itself.

With equal reason may it be urged—keep the thought off the personality as a whole. Do not let the mind sink into itself, for the self-centred state is an abnormal attitude and always a precursor of mental and physical inharmony. A large class of invalids could be cured by simply diverting their attention from themselves, for as a matter of fact their disease consists in being self-centred. They are like people who should stick their fingers into their eyes and complain of the irritation. All they have to do is to take their fingers out of their eyes. This may not be so simple as it appears, for such people are in a measure self-hypnotised, that is, they are psychologised by a fixed idea. The best method of dehypnotisation is to think of some one else and the joys and sorrows of others. Do good! Forget yourself! Take an active interest in helping some one else, and as you do this you are at the same time becoming your own friend and making an ally of your nervous system.

While right-thinking of necessity involves some attention to self, it is better accomplished by regular discipline each day in meditation and concentration of thought than in constant self-watchfulness, which becomes too introspective and tends to paralyse the mental processes; discipline, that is, with a view of forming the *habit* of right-thinking, for habit, as we shall see, may be our best ally.

Incoming currents reach the brain through the afferent nerves and are known collectively as the *afferent.* Received in a centre, they result in an outgoing current or nervous discharge through the efferent. The relation of the afferent and efferent to our general subject, however, can better be considered under the Will and is reserved for that chapter.

CHAPTER III

HABIT

THE substance of the preceding chapter reveals how closely habit is associated with the nervous system, for as habits are merely fixed ways of thinking, they must result in fixed nervous reactions and in time these reactions must induce the corresponding modes of thought. In fact, habit and the nervous system are insolubly bound together. As we wear trails by taking always one course through the woods, so we establish neural paths by fixed modes of thinking. As every one knows, the feet seem instinctively to get into the old trail, while it requires an effort to break out a new path. It is next to impossible to keep an old trail-horse out of the ruts, though the travelling may be much better one side or the other of the trail. Now neural paths have just this effect upon the stream of consciousness, affording directions of least resistance through which it may flow.

A beaten path suggests to us that we follow it, whereas otherwise it might never occur to us to go in that direction at all.

Almost everything we do, from wearing clothes and cooking our food to reading books or controlling our thoughts, is a matter of habit. One becomes dependent upon smoking or drinking; stop either for a while and the very taste for these disappears. Whatever we do often, we incline to do more; whatever we desist from, we have, as time goes on, less and less inclination for. We have no better friends than good habits and no greater foes than our bad habits. With the latter we are less concerned here than with the former, for good habits are an auxiliary to both our mental and physical life and as a good habit implies a normal attitude to that particular relation, whatever it may be, the nervous reactions are normal and healthful as well.

As for bad habits, the best way to overcome them is to starve out their root-ideas in mind. Acquire the habit of ignoring them until they die for lack of recognition, as die they must. Meanwhile supplant the false idea with a true one by persistent cultivation. While this is easier said than done, it is done in this way to far better advantage than by the usual method of combating the thing to be overcome. For to combat is to meet with greater resistance. The idea of non-resistance in this connection is good psychology. Things have that power over us which we give them; they have no power in themselves. Their importance to us depends altogether upon the rank we give them in our own consciousness. One cannot do without his cup of coffee, a second without his cigar, a third without champagne. But what are these things to an Esquimaux, who would miss nothing so much as the blubber to which he is accustomed? Do not fight with your ill-considered habits; learn to ignore them by concentrating the attention on something else. To fight is to give them greater importance in consciousness and thus to increase their seeming power. Instead, minimise that power while asserting your own superiority and cultivating true friends to take the place of the false ones. Seek the angels and you need not resist the devils; but you must cultivate the angels with all the persistence and devotion you once gave to thc devils. When you have formed a good habit, not only will it become necessary to you but the bad habit will no longer appeal and will die a natural death. A new set of neural paths are thus formed, while the old paths are gradually obliterated.

Good habits are so many lieutenants, working for us by relieving us of conscious attention to many details. Compare the efforts of a child learning to walk, or of a man learning to swim or to ride the bicycle, with the skipping boy or the expert swimmer or bicyclist, and you have a good example of what habit may do, for walking, swimming, and riding are merely habits. Now our conscious mental processes—as far as the habit of right-thinking is concerned—are often as ineffective as the efforts of the child to walk or of the beginner on the bicycle. Suppose we were obliged to make the same effort in breathing that we do in voluntary action, how laborious it would be. Thus controlled thinking is an effort at first, but once let it become a habit and it goes on almost automatically thenceforth. In this connection we can hardly lay too much emphasis on the importance of habit. To make your habit friendly is at the same time to make your nervous system an ally The expert bicyclist rides without the least thought of his machine, but it was not until riding became a habit that it ceased to be a conscious process with him. In the same way an expert thinker would come in time to balance his mind and largely to control it in accordance with the laws of right-thinking, with little or no conscious attention either to his body or to the mental processes themselves.

With most of us, wrong-thinking is habitual and automatic. When right-thinking becomes automatic and as unconscious as breathing, we shall have become truly our own friends. The heart beats and the lungs are inflated without conscious effort and the muscles are never tired, whereas voluntary action of the muscles soon fatigues. Athletes who persist too long in the development of any set of muscles become muscle-bound. Too much conscious direction of thought produces a sort of mental paralysis: we become thought-bound. There must be an outlet in action; it must find expression because of that intimate association of thought and the nervous system to which reference has so frequently been made. If it does not, we become self-hypnotised by watching our own mental processes. Mere affirmations are not sufficient in themselves. One who goes no further than this is like a would-be bicyclist who should devote his energies to affirming he could ride, without ever getting on a machine to give his thought outlet in action. If you affirm you are free from the tyranny of sensation, lose no opportunity of proving it to yourself. Endeavour to give concrete expression to the truths you hold in mind, for only so do they become galvanised into life.

Kindness, consideration, cheerfulness, self-forgetfulness and self-control may all become habits. They should in fact be designated the normal habits of a thoroughbred mentality, as they are the normal inheritance of the spiritually well-born. They are acquired, perhaps, painfully at first and with much effort. But consider the balance, the poise, the efficiency of the expert rider and that, furthermore, all this is the result of habit. Riding at ease, he is free to enjoy the landscape, with no thought of himself; while the beginner, with eyes riveted on his machine, flounders about the road in momentary dread of falling on his head. In like manner the habit of right-thinking relieves us from conscious effort or from attention to the mental processes or to the body, while we may go on our way well-balanced and free to look about us and enjoy the panorama of life.

In regard to the method of acquiring these habits, a word should be said about inhibition.

While we may attend to directing some thought currents, they are often offset by incoming currents of an undesirable character. It is here we should inhibit by giving the negative thought no recognition. Put down the brakes! Stop thinking! Then turn into another road. To inhibit is merely to put on the brakes. We steer by our understanding of the road and our knowledge of the country —in this case the laws of right-thinking. The efficient instrument for accomplishing this is the Will.

CHAPTER IV

THE WILL

WE have seen that sense impressions of the outer world come to the mind through the afferent, a mechanism purely automatic in its working and alike in man and the ape. In the lower animals—virtually machines—all their activities are comparable with that which is involuntary with us. Nothing intervenes between the afferent impression and the efferent result. The will does not exist. Titillate the nerve of a decapitated frog and the frog will kick precisely as if alive, and this action illustrates the conduct of purely afferent people. A particular stimulus results in a nervous discharge, which may be motor in effect, as when the drunkard, seeing a bottle, lifts it to his lips, or when we react upon prejudices aroused by the mere sight of certain things and immediately express annoyance or anger.

In man the will normally intervenes between the afferent and the efferent, and where it does not, it is because it is either atrophied, or the action has become a habit and the will is not called upon at all. This is the case with bad habits when sufficiently indulged, and the effect upon the will is that it becomes flaccid like an unused muscle. For the will is strengthened by use precisely as muscles are developed by exercise. Neither is the will called upon in an established good habit, as, for instance, the habit of right-thinking; but it is by means of the will in the first place that we are able to form that habit. Thus we may say that good habits are formed by the will, while bad habits are in large measure the result of an ineffective will.

Will, then, is energy, and its function is not only to intervene between incoming and outgoing currents but to give force to motives and resolves. We may form good resolutions, but they are of no use unless we have the will to carry them out. Character may be defined as a will acting in accordance with wisdom. More than any other factor, the will gives force and identity to the personal self, and whatever influences tend to weaken the will are of necessity bad. If, as its enemies claim, hypnotism has this effect, it is certainly to be avoided. It is obvious, however, that the will is not sufficient in itself. If we choose between two roads or two courses of action, our choice is the result of such wisdom as we have, but we must will to choose and again will to pursue the course we have chosen. Strangely enough some psychologists, like Spencer, make nothing of the will, while others overestimate its office. Suffice it to say that the will is efficient only as it is intelligently directed.

In building the acquired areas in the brain, the instrument is the will. For example, in developing a music centre through cultivation of that art, it is by the energy of the will that we work and study and persevere. It is the will to work, the will to learn, the will to do, that is ever fashioning our brains, our mentalities, in accordance with specific ideals. The will does not supply those ideals, however. In relation to the nervous system, it will readily be seen that the will must be a powerful modifier of nervous reactions. Suppose, for instance, you see something that arouses your indignation, and, without any intervention of the will, you allow it to find efferent expression in a fit of anger. The stream of consciousness is swept, as it were, by a hurricane, the motor centres are inhibited from doing their automatic work, the viscera are more or less disturbed, pulse and respiration change and acids are created in the blood and secretions. As a result you are mentally and physically upset. Suppose, on the other hand, the will strongly interfered after the afferent impression which was the occasion of all this, and in time to check the rising storm, the resulting nervous reactions would thus be mitigated or avoided.

We should aim, therefore, to let the will and not the afferent be the agent of our acts except where, in the case of useful habits, we have disciplined ourselves to act wisely without conscious effort. The pupil must for a long time will to hold his bow correctly in learning the violin, but with the virtuoso this has become automatic and he gives it no thought. If, however, he had not first disciplined himself, he would have acquired bad habits of bowing and to overcome these would then necessitate a great effort of the will.

The efficient means of strengthening the will is to lose no opportunity of putting good resolutions into practice. Will to do a useful thing and then *do* it. Confront every afferent impression with the resolute will and await the dictates of reason before acting. You may thus determine what mental state and virtually what nervous reactions, if any, shall ensue. In impulsive natures, the time between an afferent impression and its efferent discharge is very brief, while with phlegmatic temperaments it is much longer. It amounts to the same thing, however, unless the will performs its office. One is an electric spark, the other a slow fuse. The advantage of the slow reaction is that there is more time in which the will may act. The theory of the will is quite simple and, like a theory of physical development, is of no use whatever unless it is put into practice. Reading about exercise never gives any one strength. The advantage of reading, or of watching others, is that it may inspire one to do something for himself.

An emission of the will is virtually a prayer that the particular things willed shall come to pass, and in this sense willing is praying. The will to do right may become a habit; that is, a rightly developed will may become habitual, and this sets in motion psychic activities as yet little understood. The directed will is not only efficient energy in itself but is reinforced from the universal energy, whereas the weak and inefficient will is further weakened by currents of negation from the world-thought. The will to work, and better still the will to do good work, is for all practical purposes the prayer of the workman, and this prayer finds answer in the quality of the work itself. Will to amount to something, will to succeed in your life-work, and work at your task, assured that your prayer will be answered. But go at your work in a half-hearted, indifferent way, let your will be weak, your energy misdirected, and all your prayers to the empty sky will not avail you in the least.

It is evident that the will, thus considered, is merely the instrument of our activities. It is, in a sense, force. As to how we use that force, whether wisely or unwisely, will depend on our intelligence. Our finite vision is limited and unreliable; we see but the minutest arc of the perfect circle, and it follows that the highest use of the will is to adapt the mind to the purposes of that Higher Will we name God. We do not and can not always know what is best even for ourselves. Our worldly wisdom is often folly. Sufficient reason then that we should aim, not to act of ourselves so much as to let the Supreme Will act through us. As we have seen, the Soul is in truth God in us—the unchangeable background over which passes the ever changing stream of consciousness. To merge the human will in the Divine is simply to bring the Soul into consciousness, and to do this is to think and act in accordance with Principle. In our opposition to Truth we are as a machine out of gear, an instrument out of tune, a discord, and our action becomes mal-action.

The "will of God" is sanity and peace and health, and in so far as we express these we reflect the true purpose of life. We are nothing; God is all. Our life is in God, our energy is of God, and the human will is intended, not to obstruct, but to admit the tide of power from above. Its supreme function is to place us in the divine current that it may act through us, that instead of the fruitless effort to supply, we shall be in position to fully receive the energy.

CHAPTER V

ATTENTION

MANY influences play upon the mind at any given moment and several factors determine to which we shall give attention, such as interest, habit, will, and nervous conditions. Chief among these are interest and habit, and the attention is as a rule alive to a thing in proportion to the interest we have in it, so that in looking over a newspaper we detect at a glance the item which most concerns our peculiar and personal interest among a mass of wholly irrevelant matter. In a flash we see the stock quotation, the name of a friend, the reference to country or city with which we are familiar. Women instantly see details of dress which a man would never detect. Let a naturalist, an artist, and a merchant walk together through the woods and they will receive three distinct sets of impressions corresponding to the particular interests of each. The naturalist will be alive to birds and plants, the artist to colour effects and composition, and the merchant to real-estate and lumber possibilities. The artist will not see the most obvious commercial value, while the merchant will be blind to the plants under foot and deaf to the birds overhead. Each has acquired the habit of looking for that in which he is interested to the exclusion of other things.

What applies to normal tastes applies equally to abnormal ones. People who constantly attend to physical conditions in themselves or their children are keenly alive to minute changes of air, details of diet, and possible dangers which do not even occur to those who are differently constituted. Self-centred persons also are attentive to subtle conditions with reference to themselves which others do not notice. Habit and interest work together to make us sensitive to certain impressions. The more we pay attention to any particular class of ideas, the more attentive we become. It is thus, the naturalist becomes so good an observer, the engineer so alive to the condition of his engine, the musician so sensitive to discord, tone, and technic. Fear is also one of the mainsprings of attention with many, and to be afraid of diseases or burglars or drafts is to be always looking for them, to be keenly attentive in these several directions. Thus is formed the habit of looking for undesirable things—of never *over*looking them—a habit which plays havoc with the nervous system.

We can have but a superficial idea of any subject if the interest has not been aroused, for only then do we become attentive, and the moment we become attentive the subject begins to grow in our consciousness, and to assume new proportions and a different aspect. Unless we are truly observant we may look at a thing and never see it. This fact of psychology is as beneficial in one way as it may be harmful in another. Consider the details to which confirmed invalids give attention and how unprofitable such things appear to a robust person. Consider the things which frighten little children and timid people and how remote these are from the consciousness of a strong man. The question is then, to some extent, to what class of things do you *choose* to attend, and to what class will you be indifferent? For this choice persisted in will form a habit, and to have the habit of always being receptive to the good, the beautiful, and the true, but deaf and blind to the false and mean, is to build upon a rock.

Men pay little heed to spiritual and philosophic truth because their interest is so absorbed in other directions, in business and worldly affairs. It is usually when in trouble or in fear of losing their health that they turn for the first time to spiritual things. They will thus repeat dogmas for years which they do not in the least comprehend and which have no meaning for them whatever, simply because like a parrot repeating the same thing, they have given no attention to the subject. The moment they do wake up and attend to it, the absurdity of some of their beliefs becomes evident to them.

Nothing, for instance, can be more vital than a knowledge of the working of our minds —a practical psychology—yet how few have awakened to any interest in this subject. Having no interest they are not attentive, and the most obvious facts and relations concerning mental action pass unnoticed by those who, having eyes, see not; for they have no eyes as yet for this particular thing. When one first becomes interested in helping himself through a better understanding and a more efficient control of his mental forces, he will be astonished that simple facts which then become evident should have for so long escaped his attention. And if the interest is sincere, he will be equally surprised at the magnitude which that interest will presently assume, and at the number of corrections he will have to make in his previous opinions.

In this connection it must occur to him that a good part of his energy has been wasted through the habit of wandering in his mind, that is by a scattered attention and by lack of discrimination. He will find that he has given much attention to unprofitable things, such as his aches and pains, the shortcomings and peculiarities of others, and the bridges which he may have to cross but which in all probability he never will. The mind is not unlike an unruly horse which needs to be tamed and held well in hand. When the horse shies or prances in fear he must be calmed and reassured. If he starts to run he must be held in with a firm hand. If he balks be must be urged along. In short he must be disciplined with firmness and good judgment until he becomes a well-broken animal. A mind which has never been disciplined is like the fractious horse, a constant source of trouble. The foolish horse shying at objects in the road, simply because they attract his eye, typifies the state of the undisciplined mind.

When this is once perceived, the next step is to eliminate the unprofitable things from consciousness by withdrawing the thought from them and concentrating it upon that type of impressions and that class of ideas which are profitable—upon truth, that is, and not upon error. Subdue the mind into following the road which reason directs and at the pace which the will enjoins. Concentration is no more than an absorbed attention. You will find people have great powers of concentration when they are watching a fire or a ball game; they have very little when it comes to reflecting upon philosophy. That same singleness of purpose and focusing of the mind which goes to the ball game would work wonders if applied every day to establishing mental control and picturing true ideas.

Concentration is not only a good mental exercise but is essential to mental efficiency. Uncontrolled force of any kind is for the most part wasted. To focus the attention, like converging the rays of the sun, is to derive added power, provided the thought is directed upon a proper object. The ill effects of misdirected attention are shown in cases of intense grief and fear and in monomania. Truth is the normal field of activity, and just here we have the basis of Suggestion, which will be considered in a later chapter. That upon which we focus the attention stands out in relief, as in the field of a searchlight, while all else is in darkness. Let that concentration fall upon Absolute Truth and error has no existence for that mind—as it has no reality in fact; but let it fall upon error, and truth is for the time non-existent for that person. It is evident that discrimination is quite as important as attention. We must concentrate upon that which is true and remove the attention from that which is false.

CHAPTER VI

IMAGINATION

THE stream of consciousness may be likened to a series of moving pictures. We may be said to think in images. Not all of these, however, are visual, for they may be auditory, verbal, and even muscular. Thus we may mentally hear the sound of words, or in thinking them we may have the bodily feeling of them in the vocal organs. We may have a visual picture of a man running, or we may, in thinking of the runner, have the bodily feeling of running ourselves. Picture yourself in a hundred-yard dash and see if you do not have a feeling of it in your legs and in the head and shoulders as well. If the picture is vivid, there will be the feeling of pushing the shoulder forward as if to get over the line. Fancy yourself to be stroking the Varsity crew and you will have in the back and arms the bodily feeling of rowing.

The association is thus very close between a mental picture and a corresponding bodily state—one of the most important facts of psychology in the relation of mind and body. Some think largely in verbal, some in visual, others, like musicians, in auditory images. Whichever it may be, thought frames itself always in an image of some kind; presumably, in most minds, in that most appropriate to the character of their thought.

With the half-educated, imagination is merely the synonym for delusion. But the truth is that the imaging faculty is essential to thought, for we cannot escape the necessity of thinking in images of some sort. Imagination is properly a recollection and association of former mental images and it may be a faithful reproduction or a recombination of the original elements into a purely fanciful picture. It is that faculty without which there would be neither Literature nor Art; but, like everything else, it works good or harm according as it is directed or misdirected, used or abused. There are diseased imaginations as there are morbid emotions. Yet emotion and imagination are good in themselves and essential to our thought-life. The thing is to make friends of our own faculties. Make an ally of the imagination by drawing only true pictures, or at least those which are agreeable and wholesome. That which applies to thinking applies to the imaging of thought. Give no room to morbid or unwholesome pictures, for as the original thought gave rise to nervous reactions, so may a replica produced long after result in similar reactions.

It is this fact, particularly, which concerns us here. The image in which we think seems more tangible than the mind-stuff of which that image is formed and it is easier to deal with it for that reason. Much depends upon the clearness and vividness of the mental picture, and, little as we understand the inner process, we may at least affirm that wherever emotion is associated with the imaging process the picture will be more lasting. This is particularly true of images formed in great fear, for these appear to be stamped much more deeply than others. Mere fanciful pictures may have no more permanence than negatives which have not been "fixed" and which fade on being exposed to the light. When a picture is formed under the stress of emotion, however, the emotion appears to act like a fixing bath and to give the negative permanence. Thus pictures of accidents have been known to persist many years and after the lapse of time to still produce physical distress on occasion. These pictures may be hung on the walls of memory, or they may have been relegated to that little known region the subconscious, where, although they are forgotten, their presence not even suspected, they still have power to induce nervous reactions consonant with those they originally produced when fresh in mind.

This relation of mental images to the body, when formed during an emotional state, is peculiar and very subtle. Professor James quotes an instance in which a gentleman, having accidentally crushed his child's finger in the door, himself experiences for several days thereafter acute pain in his own finger. Mr. Whipple cites many cases showing the relation of pictures formed in childhood or youth to diseases which manifested themselves in after life. The moral is—to create no negative pictures; and where, as in the case of accidents, such pictures are formed in spite of us, not to dwell upon them afterward, as is usually done, but to begin at once to eliminate them by some healthful thought process calculated to that end. Let the will assert itself at once to restore equilibrium and to persistently erase, as it were, the undesirable image, while outlining and fixing in its place one of calmness and peace. This will be easier in proportion as we have cultivated the habit of creating harmonious pictures and of rejecting those which portray discord. Newspaper crimes and patent medicine advertisements form negative pictures in the mind of the reader. To think or talk of disease or crime is to make the mind more and more susceptible to negative images. Avoid those people who habitually talk of these things. They are disease-mongers.

It is a peculiarity of the imagination that it engenders emotion. Thus if some one has offended us, when we afterwards recall the incident and bring to mind the picture of his offensive conduct, we experience again the feeling of indignation, and the more we think of it, the more indignant we become. It is as if, having once outlined a picture lightly in pencil, we should every now and then go over it again until the lines were cut into the paper. Obviously it grows more and more difficult to erase such a picture. Of the several classes, visual images appear to impress themselves more deeply and to be more prepotent in nervous reactions, perhaps because they have greater appearance of reality. The more reality we give to a picture, the more harm we may experience if it is negative, the more good if positive. If you have escaped from anything, be thankful and think no more about it. Sever your connection with it in consciousness as soon as possible. The affair actually lasted but a few moments, it may be, but by creating a vivid picture to store in the subconscious, it may virtually be made to last as long as you live, and over and over again to engender the same emotions. After a while emotions may cease, but the nervous reactions will continue from habit.

Through suggestion it is possible to create negative images in the minds of others. In the case of physicians this is inexcusable, and those who to-day are so ignorant of the psychology of the imagination and the emotions, or of the nature of suggestion, as to thus endanger their patients are unfit to practise. In their ignorance they do more harm than they can ever do good. The minds of the sick are often especially receptive to negative images. Sickness is almost always associated with fear. The anxious mind of the patient is like a sensitised paper upon which the doctor's verdict produces a picture of the very disease the patient fears. Mental images created under stress of fear can not fail to produce nervous reactions of an unfavourable character. Wholly aside from the merits or demerits of medication the physician should be a practical psychologist; and nothing is more important than that he should always approach his patients with the intention of creating in their minds pictures of hope, courage, wholeness. Never should he emphasise the thought of disease. Now it is the very stock in trade of the quack to create in the mind of his victim a picture of the disease to which the patient considers himself liable. Every patent medicine advertisement is carefully designed to do this in accordance with principles of psychology. If you have strong and robust lungs, you may read of pulmonary troubles without its making any impression, for you do not in the least apply what you read to yourself. If, however, you have a deep-rooted fear that your lungs may become diseased because your father's were, the effect of your reading may be quite different. Whatever fear we entertain makes us sensitive in that direction and susceptible to influences which would otherwise have no power.

As far as the imagination is concerned, the mind may be regarded as a picture gallery in which are hung these psychic pictures, and the importance of the subject is far from being wholly utilitarian and a matter of physical results. The condition of the mind itself is affected by the kind of images it entertains. Consider what would be the result, for instance, of filling your house with pictures of gruesome and unpleasant subjects at which you were obliged to look from morning till night. Yet that is precisely the condition of the unfortunate person whose mental gallery is filled with images of inharmony and disease. Consider, on the other hand, the effect of beautiful pictures in your house—fine landscapes, pastoral scenes, heroic figures, noble faces, and types of physical beauty and perfection—and you have an example of a highly cultivated moral and æsthetic nature in which normal ideals are the dominant factors. The images in such a mind are of purity, strength, and beauty, and the personal self is to that extent in harmony with the Soul which is itself Truth and Beauty absolute.

CHAPTER VII

EMOTION

EVERY emotion is composed of a mental state and a nervous reaction, which induce in turn a state of mind more complex than the first. Thus if a shock occasions fright, we experience the usual effect upon the heart and the respiration and these sensations tend to augment the original sense of fear. If we are embarrassed and cough or gape, the coughing and gaping may increase the embarrassment. If an annoyance causes us to lose our temper, the bodily feeling of anger makes us all the more angry. Our emotions are never disembodied and their nervous reactions are far more pronounced than is the case with purely intellectual concepts. In fact there are few things about which the mind engages itself—even of an unemotional character in themselves—which do not tend to arouse some emotion in us.

There are so many notes on our emotional keyboard, from pride and envy to love and benevolence, that we are quite certain to strike one or another. We do almost nothing impersonally. Even if we absolutely put ourselves aside, we are apt to feel pride or self-pity at the very fact that we have put ourselves aside. Our thought-life is thus completely bound up with the emotions, and because of their nervous reactions they play an important part in keeping us well, or in creating disorder.

People differ greatly, it goes without saying, in the character and intensity of their emotions. Distinctly emotional natures discharge feeling on the slightest provocation, or without provocation. With some, both fear and anger are out of all proportion to the motives which give rise to them. Such people wear out the mechanism of the emotions by constantly playing on them and become irritable and nervous. They are like hotel pianos which everybody takes a turn at, with the result that the tone is soon cracked and they are always out of tune. Colder natures, on the other hand, are slow in their emotional responses. Nervous reactions are sudden and perhaps more violent with the first class, but not necessarily so deep or so prolonged in their effect as with those minds which, slow to feel, still persist in any feeling once aroused. The tendency of modern life is to over-stimulate the emotions, to keep them keyed up, so that we become emotional topers and nervous wrecks. The emotions are not normally intended to be in constant use. Such a state, both dissipated and vulgar, is fostered in some by the newspapers in their persistent effort to show everything in an emotional light and to make the most stupid commonplaces dramatic. The chief cause is the complexity of our social life to-day, and the increased absorption in ideas which are material and emotional, to the exclusion of all ideas which are contemplative and philosophic. The cure for it is intellectual and spiritual cultivation, simpler living, and both deeper and higher thinking.

In place of classifying the emotions, we may simply divide them for our purpose into those which are negative and those which are positive in their reactions. Fear, anger, and grief are as deleterious in their effect on the nervous system, and thence on the body, as love and all kindred emotions are beneficent. It will be seen that what has been said on the influence of thought applies to the subject of the emotions, for it is the same thing whether we call it the emotion of fear in the abstract, or whether we call it a fearful or anxious thought. The thing to be borne in mind is that whenever emotion is related to our train of thought, the nervous reactions are more acute. An emotion is indeed partly physical inasmuch as it is a mental state mixed with a bodily feeling. We not only feel sorry but we feel a lump in the throat; we feel not only angry, but likewise we feel all the bodily agitation that goes with that state. A "bodily feeling" is of course a mental state directly induced by the body.

Among the immediate results of the nervous changes which follow emotional states are dryness of the throat, flushing or pallor, suffocation, perspiration, acceleration or retardation of the heart action, indigestion, disturbance in the functions of the liver, the kidneys, the bowels, and the bladder, together with chemical changes in the blood and in the secretions. We have no exact knowledge of why this takes place or to what extent it does so, but any one can by observing himself verify it in some particulars at least. The reactions vary with the temperament, the will, the intelligence, and with the mental and physical state at any given time. We are more susceptible at one time than at another. But we may confidently affirm that the results of negative emotions are always unhealthful, while the reverse are beneficial. To be cheerful or kind, gentle, serene, and patient always reacts favourably. Every kind thought, every courageous thought, every pure thought is a good investment for the nervous system, for the body as well as for the mind. We may meet a catastrophe without unfavourable result if we can keep fear out of the mind; on the other hand, we may experience bad effects from a false alarm if we give way to fear.

While the emotions are not readily subject to control, the tendency should be to cultivate those which are positive and beneficial and discourage as far as possible all that are negative. Make it the rule of your life to hold fast to love and let go of fear. The practice of such a rule must tend to form a habit, so that you will become less and less subject to fear and more and more amenable to love. Now there are many variations of fear, such as worry, anxiety, envy, jealousy, selfishness, and malice, while love expresses itself in kindness, gentleness, patience, considerateness, and tolerance.

The ideal state, then, is to be calm, allowing the stream of consciousness to be coloured only by the beneficent emotions, and inhibiting the negative states as soon as they appear. Since there is always action and reaction and the flesh induces states of mind through suggestion, "assume a virtue if you have it not" and it will help you to that end. Look calm even if you do not feel so; smile and it will help you to be cheerful; throw out the chest and breathe deeply and you will sooner overcome your fear. To be ever watching ourselves and our emotions would be tedious enough; yet if we do not we shall be caught napping, unless, indeed, we have formed the habit of giving room to the positive emotions only, and again habit is our best ally—an ally who watches over us while we sleep.

It is here that the limitations of psychology become evident, for while it may reveal to us the relation of emotive states to nervous changes and organic functions, if we ask Why should we not grieve, or fear calamity, or why should we love our neighbour? we must turn to religion, to philosophy, and to ethics for our answer. Yet the practical disclosures of psychology will be found to be in accord with the higher revelations of religion and philosophy. We are not to grieve, because life is the one and only reality and death is but a seeming. Form changes, the stream of consciousness changes, because it is in the nature of things and was so ordained, but the self as knower—the Soul—which is God in us does not change. It was not born; it will not die. Grieve not then over the unreal and temporal but cleave to the real and eternal. We are not to fear because whatever pertains to the cosmic order is best, and whatever proceeds from our own lives is the result of our thought processes and, if undesirable, can be overcome by reversing the process and supplementing truth for error in our own minds. We are not to fear, for we have no life of our own; our life is in God and God is Love. Love is the one reality of the universe and whatever is not in accordance with love is not of God, but is illusion, and has only that power and that seeming life which we give it in consciousness.

CHAPTER VIII

BELIEF

THAT there is a ground of absolute truth underlying the sea of opinions is the fundamental tenet of spiritual philosophy What we think of this truth does not affect the truth itself but it does affect us, and this is the keynote of what may be said on the subject of Belief.

No category could contain the beliefs which mankind entertains. It would be impossible to enumerate even the series of beliefs of the average man in the course of a lifetime. The stream of consciousness flows through a variety of landscapes in its ever-changing bed, dominated by beliefs, or, let us say, concepts—for a belief is merely a concept for which we assume verity. The stream, now shallow, anon deeper, now broad, again narrow, is turbulent or placid, swift or slow. To-day we believe one thing, to-morrow another, and next year something else, but Truth itself is unchangeable. Every one is provided with a set of hygienic beliefs and of religious, moral, social, and personal beliefs. Some of these affect us but slightly, lying in fields to which we give little attention; while others, personal in their nature, take a deep hold, arouse the emotions and excite nervous reactions. It is this class which play a prominent part in our thought-life and have a marked influence upon both character and health.

Whatever we believe to be so, is virtually so to us while we entertain that opinion. Having accepted it as fact, although it may be fiction, the idea thus held in mind and its psychic picture are capable of producing the customary reactions. The mental process is the same if the belief be true or if it be false. A certain type of supposed action is in reality entirely a reaction on our part. Thus if a bear attacks you there is both action and reaction, but if you mistake a stump for a bear and run, there has been only a reaction on your part—the stump has done nothing. It was not the stump, but your fear of the stump—that is to say, your belief—which was active. In many of our beliefs we ascribe action and power in this way, whereas it is our belief alone which is active and the object of such belief has no more power than the stump in the illustration. It is a keen eye that can always distinguish a stump from a bear in the dusk, and it is a wise man who can tell truth from error in the perpetual dusk which ignorance casts over the world.

So vast is the conflicting mass of opinions to which the religious and intellectual life of man has given rise that many have assumed everything to be a matter of opinion, that all is relative and there is no such thing as absolute truth. This is merely a false belief itself and nothing could be further from the facts. As the circumference of a circle bears a fixed relation to its diameter, irrespective of all opinions whatsoever, so man has a definite relation to God, and his life is subject to immutable laws, whatever he may or may not believe. Ignorance of the principles by which life is governed, as well as the superstitious acceptance of error for truth, of fiction for fact, is responsible for a great part of our troubles While the finite mind can never grasp Truth in its entirety, it must, in the course of human evolution, become ever increasingly aware of it. There is nothing to prevent the acquisition of spiritual or philosophic truth, any more than there was anything to prevent the development of the applied sciences—nothing, that is, but our own ignorance. The attention is focused on the material aspects of life; hence the rapid development of sciences associated with commerce. Who, from the beginning of Chemistry or of Electricity, could have predicted the present expansion of these sciences? Yet it is as absurd to deny that we can know anything of absolute Truth as it would have been to deny that we could ever know more of electricity than Franklin did, or that there was any such thing as electrical energy. The truth concerning the nature of man, his relation to God, the nature of consciousness and the reactions which follow mental processes, is as essential to the art of living, as applied science is to Commerce. If we have made relatively little progress in this direction it is because the race-mind has been otherwise engaged. Truth about these things is, it goes without saying, as fixed and unalterable as the laws which govern the motion of the heavenly bodies; and while the false concepts of the race can never affect the truth, they have a constant bearing upon the condition of mind and thence upon the bodies of those who earnestly accept them.

As in the case of the bear, many of our false concepts rest upon false percepts. We mistake a thing for something else and any conceptual state which may ensue must be infected with error. If we perceive, under the stress of emotion, we are less likely than ever to see clearly. Both love and fear act in this way. Lovers are incapable of seeing the enamoured one as others see her and no one else can see what the lover does. People in a panic of fear see what has no existence save in their own imagination. A percept, however, may be correct and the conceptual state which follows entirely false because of inability to draw proper deductions or to form logical conclusions. We are not trained to think and for the most part we have no practice in reasoning along lines not connected with our vocation. We have business shrewdness but no philosophic acumen. It is because of this we accept the most absurd statements with reference to hygiene, medicine, or theology without questioning. If any one has a fixed prejudice or false belief of long standing he comes to react upon it automatically and is almost incapable of reasoning where that prejudice is concerned, though he may be reasonable in other directions. Many an earnest Christian is incapable of reasoning about the Bible. He cannot make himself do it. But, if not a narrow bigot, he is quite able to reason about the Koran.

People who have a venerable belief in the ill effect of some particular dish find it equally difficult to reason where that is concerned, or to be more exact, they are committed to false reasoning. One declares that fish poisons him, another that it is impossible to digest potatoes, a third that cherries never agree with him. Almost every article of food is condemned by some one. None agree—least of all, the doctors. To see how spurious the usual reasoning is in regard to this subject, we have only to remember that the stomach is not a test-tube in which with given reagents definite reactions must occur. Unlike the chemical reaction, the process of digestion is complicated by mental states and is never independent of the mind The action of a given food depends upon the state of mind in which we eat it. Any food may disagree with us if taken under the stress of negative emotion, for as we have said in Chapter II, the automatic centres are inhibited by neural currents induced by injurious mental states, so that the organs which they govern cannot function normally. In view of this it is easy to see how a person, having once eaten a certain dish under such circumstances and experiencing unpleasant results, may thenceforth associate the trouble with the dish, leaving the state of mind out of the problem altogether and assuming that the dish in question disagrees with him for purely physical reasons.

The mental picture formed under these conditions derives added power from the well-recognised fact in psychology of association. If a process B follows a process A a sufficient number of times, the mind establishes a sequence between the two so that whenever A occurs, not only is a state of expectancy aroused that B will ensue, but neural paths are formed tending to that end. Thus it may happen in time A will indeed precipitate B, though there is no logical relation between the two, other than the mental association of B with A, and the tendency of nervous reactions to take place along established paths. In such a case, not A but the associational process and the neural paths are the true cause of B.

A well-established belief then, even if a wholly false concept, has power to act through the mental picture formed and the nervous change induced. If we believe a thing is injurious to us, the *belief* itself is quite sufficient to produce an injurious result, especially when associated with fear. This is by no means to declare that it is nothing but belief in any case, as there are things not intended for food which the digestive apparatus could not dispose of even if it would, and there are conditions under which human life cannot be sustained. We are dependent upon air, food, and heat—belief, or no belief. But, within reasonable limits, we should always investigate whether it is a thing or condition, or our beliefs about the thing or condition which is responsible for the reaction.

The fact that mere beliefs have power and may express themselves outwardly in the flesh serves above all to emphasise the necessity of replacing error in the mind with truth. We must make our concepts consonant with fact. To this end we must be more thoughtful, must focus the attention upon those practical aspects of psychology and philosophy, an understanding of which is essential to a spiritual life as distinct from mere existence or getting a living. It is only thus that we can clarify the mind and purge it of false concepts. Every erroneous belief which is replaced by a concept of truth is a victory which clarifies and strengthens the mind and at the same time eliminates an element of physical discord. Little by little truth is gained; one by one errors are displaced. Ignorance is the enemy of the world. Therefore aim to see clearly and love Truth for its own sake. For Truth is the saviour of mankind; it alone redeems us from error, and other than this there is nothing from which to be saved.

In the cant phraseology of the day which has unfortunately become common, you may hear now and again that some one has a "Belief," meaning thereby a physical disorder. While this is a catch phrase and often used in a meaningless way, it is seldom if ever used by an intelligent person to mean that one is ill merely because he *thinks* he is ill, and that merely thinking he is well will cure him. It is this false interpretation put upon it by the ignorant which provokes a sneer. While a highly imaginative and nervous person may be ill simply because he thinks he is ill, this holds only in such peculiar cases. The essential meaning, which applies universally to the relation of mind and body, must have become evident to the reader from the substance of the preceding pages: namely, that a false concept—and thoughts of malice or selfishness, and worries and anxieties, are false concepts in the light of eternal truth—does form a mental picture of a negative character, which, by inducing corresponding nervous reactions, expresses itself outwardly in some form of physical disorder.

Let it be remembered, on the other hand, that true concepts make for health and happiness. We are bound by ignorance; we are freed by truth.

CHAPTER IX

THE WORLD-THOUGHT

WHILE some concepts are original with us, we borrow many more, or rather they are instigated in the mind of the individual by the world-thought in which all minds function. As the atmosphere affects every barometer, so this mental atmosphere influences the individual, inducing fears and hopes and imbuing us with beliefs, which come, we know not whence, and take possession of us, we know not why, but which we usually assume to be the results of our own thinking. With regard to this, many are no more than puppets who respond to beliefs which enter their minds as the common air enters their lungs and whose emotions are thus largely induced from without. The excitement of mobs and the panic of crowds are recognised instances of this influence; epidemics, fashions, and fads as well as some part of our everyday thinking are to be laid at the same door.

We may even venture to say that the world-thought exerts a hypnosis over all individual minds. To what extent this is true, few ever dream. Examine yourself honestly as to how many of your habits and your beliefs are original with you or really belong to you because you have considered and accepted them on your own responsibility. We do certain things and think certain thoughts, simply because others do; and some of our ways antedate the most remote human ancestor and were derived from the baboon. The only original things about some people are their prejudices; everything else is a reflection of the world-thought. How many can say they have investigated the various forms of religious and medical belief for themselves and have accepted that which, after impartial comparison with others, they deemed the best? For the most part we are Baptists or Calvinists because our fathers were, and Republicans or Democrats, Allopaths or Homeopaths for the same reason. In like manner we accept the fears of newspaper reporters and village gossips and assume them to be our own. We laugh when others laugh and cry when others cry; we are puppets pulled by invisible wires.

Since the mental atmosphere in which we find ourselves is the source of much of our thinking and thence of our emotions and their attendant nervous reactions, it deserves a recognition in Psychology which it has not yet received. Nor can we properly consider the stream of consciousness without considering that source from which at least some of its activity is derived. This influence is in part telepathic. We *feel* the general elation or depression for no obvious cause. We feel the mental atmosphere of congenial or uncongenial environments before we are able to assign a reason. In financial panics and in epidemics the world-thought is coloured with fear and lies like a pall over humanity, and it requires a determined effort on the part of the individual to escape this depressing influence. The force of any telepathic communication is of course multiplied tenfold by talk and by newspaper comment and exaggeration. Minds are imbued with alarm and made receptive to just those pictures whose effect they wish to escape. Noncontagious diseases are propagated by the contagion of fear.

It must be remembered, however, that love may be communi ted as well as fear, and that health is as contagious as disease. In the race belief, the word contagion is associated only with undesirable things. But we have, now and then, epidemics of generosity, of charity, of morality, and these should imbue us with hope and courage to do our part in disseminating cheerfulness, sanity, and health. This is to be done by fixing the attention on positive states and withdrawing it from negative conditions by thinking health and courage and love and by talking about them. We may thus inject into the mental atmosphere, ideas which help to clarify, inspire, and uplift. Thoughts of calmness and strength are like oil poured upon the troubled waters. Consider the folly—the pernicious folly—of talking about diseases and habitually commenting on people's ill health, their paleness, or their leanness. Why inform one he has a cold—as is so commonly done? Do you suppose, if it is so, he does not know it? It is the one thing he is trying to forget—and yet you stupidly remind him of it and the next person he meets does the same, so that he has no chance to drop it from his mind, if he will. Or why tell him he is thin? He has probably found it out for himself and will not thank you for constantly reminding him of the fact. If you think your friend does not look well—pray keep it to yourself and do not be in such haste to tell him as if it were pleasant news. The world is insufferably stupid in this respect and the seeds of disease or discouragement and despair are unwittingly sown in timid or depressed minds day in and day out.

So common is this garrulous folly, that we must nerve ourselves against the unwise suggestions of family and friends. How shall we do it? By resolutely closing the ears to negative and discouraging comments and by dissuading people, as tactfully as may be, from indulging this silly habit. Make up your mind not to be influenced by anything they can say. Be adamant and steel to their negation and return wisdom for folly by instantly commenting on any hopeful sign in them which you may discover. It is a sad thing to send people away from you feeling depressed or unhappy, yet there are well-meaning persons who do this all the days of their lives. Well-meaning but ignorant people cause much sorrow in the world. It is a noble aim to imbue others with a new courage, a new hope, a new strength—and this is often done by a word. *You* can do it, if you will—you who are now a wet blanket to every one you meet. Choose then, whom you will serve, whether health and sanity and cheerfulness—or negation and despair! Only in this way can you atone for the harm you have already done. Stop talking disease and gossip! It were better for you that you were dumb than that you should continue this dreary prattling Make up your mind that you will discover something good about the next person you meet and that you will tell him forthwith.

A false belief is like a rascal in politics whose power is derived from the support he receives. The more general the acceptance of an erroneous concept, the greater its apparent power. This power lies not in the belief itself, but in the energy of the minds which accept and indorse it. It is merely a channel through which that energy finds escape. Granted there are no witches, no power in the evil-eye, yet when people believed in such things, the world-thought was greatly influenced by those beliefs. There are as many witches to-day as there ever were, but that false concept has died in the race-consciousness from lack of recognition and so its power has vanished. But if it is not witches, it is something else equally foolish. We are always ready to believe more or less nonsense, simply because we lack philosophic acumen, or are too busy or too indifferent to give honest thought to the subject.

The world-thought is merely the sum-total of the activities of individual minds, as the water of a lake is composed of the water of the various streams flowing into it. Some may be pure, some polluted, and the body of water will represent the average. The lake will be purest where a clear stream enters and most impure at the mouth of a polluted stream. In our relation to the world-thought, we may, like fish in a lake, take up our position at the entrance of pure streams and avoid the impure areas, and this is the only wise and normal attitude. There are pure areas in the mental sea. Seek them! Make yourself receptive to the good and the beautiful, invulnerable to the false and distorted. If you give no allegiance to a false concept coming from without, you will escape the resulting emotive states and their attendant reactions. Only that error directly affects us which we accept, though we sometimes suffer for the ignorance and folly of others.

All we can do is to keep our own minds wise and pure and every one who does this is influencing others in the same direction and doing something towards purifying the world-thought. Truth is our refuge and our strength. When all the world cry two and two make five, we must take our stand upon the eternal principle in virtue of which two and two are four. Don't be hoodwinked by numbers! The majority represents the average intelligence; thinkers are always in the minority.

Few in this age love truth for truth's sake, but every one is enamoured of his own opinion and would convert you to it. Rest assured that in nine cases out of ten it is in reality not his opinion at all but merely some phase of the world-thought which he so zealously reflects. If he had been born with a different coloured skin, he would think something else quite as readily. Put your trust not in other people's beliefs, but in Truth, for it alone is unfailing. All else changes. The nature of man, his true relation to God and to his fellows, the nature of consciousness and its motor effects and nervous reactions are the same in all times and for all men. Ascertain the facts with reference to these fundamental questions. Take your stand upon the truth, think truth and live the truth and the changing winds of opinion may blow over your head but they will no longer disturb you. But only that truth is yours which you have thought out for yourself. Reading *about* truth is not the same as realising it. Reading is not a substitute for thinking, as so many suppose, but merely an aid and an incentive to thought. Have you discovered for yourself that the earth is round, or are you prepared to believe it is flat if some one should write a treatise to prove it and the newspapers should take it up? Apply this test to your ventures in philosophic thought, determined to fortify your mind by a body of truth which you have made your very own. For only so can you resist the hypnosis of men's opinions and the constant suggestion of race-beliefs.

CHAPTER X

THE SUBCONSCIOUS

WE hear a great deal to-day about the subconscious and its relation to disease and abnormal conditions. Its importance is probably overrated by its exponents inasmuch as it is a departure in psychology, but chiefly because as yet we know very little about it. That there is a subconscious realm is beyond cavil in spite of the fact that orthodox psychology is loath to admit it. In the words of Bruce: "Here and there are to be found individual psychologists who, with the intellectual fearlessness of a William James, strike boldly from the primrose path of easy-going skepticism. But the lamentable truth remains that most psychologists are still so completely under the dominion of the concepts of the 'classical' school as to prefer, if possible, to explain away rather than investigate." But if any one will consider the great mass of evidence and especially the now famous cases of Felida X., Ansel Bourne, and Madame B. cited in the annals of Psychical Research, he must surely admit the fact that there is a department of subconscious intellectual activity in the human mind.

That this is distinct *per se* from the stream of consciousness itself—as the term *subliminal* self would imply—is not proven and does not appear as rational an explanation as that it is merely a submerged part of that stream, with which we naturally have less acquaintance than with the surface. Who, in looking at a river, thinks of the submerged water? Our consciousness of the stream is usually confined to the surface, yet we know very well that the river has depth and that something is going on beneath the surface. As it is not apparent we give thought to that alone which is visible. There is reason to suppose that the nature of the subconscious is not essentially different from what we know as consciousness, and, as far as it has a bearing on our present subject, we shall consider it here as merely the submerged part of the stream of consciousness.

One thing is certain: there is no ground for the assumption that the subconscious is identical with the self-as-knower. Whatever it may be, it pertains to the self-as-known; but it may be true that it is more susceptible to the influence of the Soul than is ordinary consciousness. Why? Simply because the surface of the stream of consciousness, like the surface of a brook, is ruffled and disturbed, while the submerged portion is more likely to be still and calm. Subconsciousness is, therefore, more susceptible to suggestion than is consciousness, which is so liable to distraction. And here it must be remembered that if the subconscious is susceptible to positive and wholesome suggestion, it may also be receptive to negative and unwholesome suggestion. It may be assumed that it is influenced by just this class of ideas from the world-thought and that it does reflect the fears and false beliefs of the mental atmosphere and retains these negative pictures.

A good account of the subconscious is that given by Frederick Myers. He says:

> The idea of a *threshold* of consciousness—of a level above which sensation or thought must rise before it can enter into our conscious life—is a simple and familiar one. The word *subliminal*—meaning "beneath the threshold"—has already been used to define those sensations which are too feeble to be

individually recognised. I purpose to extend this meaning to the term, so as to make it cover *all* that takes place beneath the ordinary threshold, or say, if preferred, the ordinary margin of consciousness—not only those faint stimulations whose very faintness keeps them submerged, but much else which psychology as yet scarcely recognises; sensations, thoughts, emotions, which may be strong, definite, and independent, but which, by the original constitution of our being, seldom merge into that *supraliminal* current of consciousness which we habitually identify with ourselves. Perceiving that these submerged thoughts and emotions possess the characteristics which we associate with conscious life, I feel bound to speak of a *subliminal* or *ultra-marginal consciousness*—a consciousness which we shall see, for instance, uttering or writing sentences quite as complex and coherent as the supraliminal consciousness could make them. Perceiving further that this conscious life beneath the threshold or beyond the margin seems to be no discontinuous or intermittent thing; that not only are these isolated subliminal processes comparable with isolated supraliminal processes (as when a problem is solved by some unknown procedure in a dream), but that also there is a continuous subliminal chain of memory (or more chains than one) involving just that kind of individual and persistent revival of old impressions and response to new ones, which we commonly call a Self—I find it permissible and convenient to speak of subliminal Selves, or more briefly of a subliminal Self. I do not indeed by using this term assume that there are two correlative and parallel selves existing always within each of us.

Rather I mean by the subliminal Self that part of the Self which is commonly subliminal; and I conceive that there may be—not only *co-operations* between these quasi-independent trains of thought—but also upheavals and alterations of personality of many kinds, so that what was once below the surface may for a time, or permanently, rise above it.

It is assumed by some that the subconscious in us is merely that phase of the cosmic mind which governs animal life and in virtue of which the lower animals carry on their automatic existence. This may be accepted, as far as it goes, without negating other theories of the subconscious, inasmuch as the activity of the lower centres in man is, in so far as it is automatic, certainly identical with the automatic activity of lower animals. In man, however, it is subject to modification by consciousness and usually to his disadvantage. The subconscious mind does govern the automatic centres and this is its normal and beneficent function; not its only function, however, for it is the subconscious which takes charge of that activity which is induced by habit, and in all our useful habits, the subliminal is our good friend and ally. "The word *subconscious*," says Professor Jastrow, "has a dubious sound; and those to whom it brings slight illumination associate it with questionable phenomena of rare occurrence and unusual significance. It should be a homely term; and its place is close to the hearth of our psychological interests." From the fact that the subconscious governs the lower centres, the natural inference is that in the course of mental evolution, the subconscious was first and that consciousness is a later product. How useful it is to us we may realise by supposing for a moment that we were obliged to voluntarily breathe or circulate the blood; or with respect to those acts which have been turned over to the subconscious, that we were obliged to consciously walk as is the case with the child in learning. The fact is we do a great deal subconsciously while the attention is otherwise engaged, relieving us of much of the monotony which would ensue if we had to watch the details of every process. In necessary and habitual acts like eating, walking, and dressing, a part at least of our activity is subconscious. It is equally true that with people who are habitually fearful or who are chronically fussy, fault-finding, or irritable, their moods have taken root in the subconscious and only become conscious when they rise above a given level.

Experiments in hypnotism indicate that the subconscious, in addition to its normal functions, has a vital relation to abnormal states as evidenced in multiple personality and attendant phenomena. This does not especially concern us here, and for our present purpose we may regard the subconscious as a certain impressionable part of ourselves which works, independent of consciousness, for or against us, in accordance with the character of the ideas impressed upon it; and that we are under the necessity of so dealing with this impressionable submerged mind that it shall act to our advantage always. In man as in the animal it is primarily in accord with the cosmic mind we call nature. Its derangement arises from the errors of the conscious mind gradually impressed upon it; precisely as the lower centres, which left to themselves function normally, may be distracted by nerve currents induced by the negative thoughts and emotions of the "thinking" brain.

As far as the subconscious is concerned purely with the automatic activity of the body, it knows better than the conscious mind and should not be interfered with. To quote Professor Jastrow again:

> Over-guidance by the higher centres thus cripples the efficiency of the work of the lower. The successful co-operation of both demands not only that the lower centres should be allowed to take fairly complete charge of as large a portion of the labour as they can efficiently direct, but that they should do so under a favourable oversight, not a "nervous" or intimidating or vacillating or too conscious one. The same holds in the process of acquisition of new facilities; and it is in part because children and young people are burdened with less of this interfering directorship of consciousness that they learn many things more quickly and more skilfully than adults.

In other words—take your mind off yourself!

When it comes to the realm of ideas—take care of consciousness and the subconscious will take care of itself. If, however, the subconscious has been vitiated by past erroneous thinking, as a pool is polluted by impure streams flowing into it, it is obviously necessary to check these incoming streams and substitute clear ones until the pool is in time clarified. Impress the subconscious with the ideas of purity, of righteousness, of love, and of health and sanity, that it may come to react upon these and these alone.

In conclusion, as with habit, emotion, imagination, and the nervous system, we must aim to so live and to think that the subconscious shall serve our true interest as it normally should. The means of accomplishing this lies in the power of auto-suggestion.

CHAPTER XI

SUGGESTION

IT is now generally recognised that suggestion is a psychic force by which one mind is capable of impressing another, and, through the subconscious which governs the lower centres, of altering and correcting physiological processes. At the same time the fact does not appear to be appreciated by its earnest advocates that suggestion is well-nigh universal, that we are continually subject to a hailstorm of suggestion, and that it may be either good or ill in its effect, according to the nature of the suggestion and the receptivity of the individual to that particular class of ideas. The world-thought, the people we come in contact with, the newspapers and books we read, sights we behold, to say nothing of the reflex action of our own mental states, suggest to us, and it is by reason of such character and intelligence as we possess that we consider one class of ideas and dismiss another.

A saloon suggests to a sot that he take a drink and immediately arouses his thirst; it has no such effect upon a well-balanced mind or upon one who dislikes liquor, for such a mentality is not susceptible in that direction. This common example serves as well as any could to illustrate both the method and limitation of unconscious suggestion. If you are a naturalist, the sight of a bird inspires a certain train of ideas, whereas it suggests nothing at all to a business man indifferent to bird-study. Similarly descriptions of crime and vice have an influence upon the receptive minds of the criminal and vicious, or such as are predisposed that way, but no such effect upon normal and balanced minds. By a process of discrimination and attention, practical minds invite practical suggestions, poetic minds, poetic suggestions, sensual minds, sensual suggestions, sick minds, invalid suggestions, and healthy minds those of health.

By habit, the impression of the subconscious, and the establishment of neural paths, we thus become more receptive to one class of suggestions than to another. Through conscious and directed efforts, however, any mind may be made less susceptible to one class of ideas and increasingly receptive to an entirely different class. This is what happens when a man is seen to reform and ennoble his character; and he is not much of a man who has not done this at some time in his life and is not still doing it to some extent. He simply becomes enamoured of a new set of ideas, more wholesome and beautiful or more charitable and unselfish than his previous ones, and begins suggesting them to himself until his field of consciousness is dominated by them and his character and personality show the result. Very likely the change is first suggested to him by something external to himself—a person or a book. Good men and women and good books thus sow seeds of regeneration in receptive minds which, under the stimulating effect of auto-suggestion, may develop and bear fruit in turn. In so far as the stream of consciousness may be said to be fixed at all, it is the character of the man which establishes the banks through which his thought shall flow. If that character be strong and pure, he need have little fear that adverse suggestion shall alter the course of the stream of consciousness.

Thus the power of suggestion is merely the power of thought to arouse mental response.

Its application to therapeutics lies in the fact that, as consciousness is motor and every thought results in a nervous reaction, suggestion may be wisely framed and consciously directed toward a definite end. Both mental and physical regeneration may thus be accomplished by suggestion. If I meet you on the street and merely suggest to you that you look very well, that you appear in perfect condition, that you are the picture of health, my suggestion is not without effect—whether audible or mental. And if I suggest to you that you look pale and thin and show symptoms of organic disease, you will undoubtedly feel worse for it, though you may have no disease whatever. There may have been no sufficient ground for either of the above suggestions, but the fact remains that a mere suggestion has some power in itself depending upon the force of the thought and the receptivity of the mind to that class of ideas.

Now the science of suggestion lies in directing this power in accordance with fundamental truths of philosophy and psychology, that they may be brought into expression in mind and body. The energy of thought may be compared to the energy of electricity, which unharnessed is wasteful and destructive but when controlled by science and directed in accordance with the laws of mechanics, of optics, and acoustics, serves so admirably the interests of man.

> It may be fairly asked [says Dr. Mason], has it been definitely established by experiments thoroughly carried out, that the mind can control physical, physiological processes in the body—the process, for instance, of digestion or lactation? Can it cause a blister to be raised upon sound and healthy skin without the application of any irritant or any medicinal substance whatever? These are test examples and they have all been successfully carried out under the supervision of perfectly honest and competent witnesses, many of them under my own observation and treatment.
>
> A principle, then, is here established. The mind can be so concentrated upon a physiological process as to stimulate that process to unusual activities, so as to produce curative effects, and even to superabundant activity, so as to produce pathological effects or disease. . . . The powerful effect of suggestion, especially in the hypnotic condition, is in this manner fully demonstrated. It is a fact, and a fact of greater significance and greater value as a curative agent simply, than any other single fact in the recent history of therapeutics. For, not only is it curative in physical ailments, but also in mental and moral deficiencies and criminal tendencies.

We are here concerned with suggestion only,

not with hypnotism; but whatever may be said for or against the latter, it must be admitted that it has contributed to our knowledge of the relation of mind and body and that it has established telepathy as a fact; just as we must admit that the study of the pathology of the brain and nervous system has certainly afforded us additional proofs of the power of the mind over the organs of the body and their several functions which could not easily have been arrived at in any other way.

Referring to hypnotism once more in this connection, it should be understood, that in suggestion as used by the exponents of mental healing there is no effort whatever to impress one will upon another or to control in any way the will of the patient. The true metaphysician does not *will* you to do anything, nor does he endeavour in the least to make his own personality dominant to yours. Rather does he aim to keep his relation free from the influence of personal motives. It is not he, nor his point of view, nor his personal bias which is to influence and benefit the patient, but that impersonal truth to which he acts merely in the capacity of an instrument in framing and suggesting it to the patient's mind. And he can honestly affirm as his attitude to those he essays to benefit: "The words that I speak unto you I speak not of myself: but the Father that dwelleth in me, He doeth the works," or in philosophic language—"The truth shall free the mind from its false beliefs and establish normal reactions in the body as a result. I suggest truth to you with the knowledge that when this truth itself possesses your mind and replaces the error, it must manifest itself outwardly." Let it be clearly understood that in the New Thought, to cure a mental or physical trouble means to *remove* the cause and not merely to make one temporarily oblivious to it, by changing the current of thought. The cause may be moral and in that case moral regeneration is the only cure. As long as a false belief is entertained, so long is the nervous system liable to the particular reaction which that state of mind induces. You have cured nothing by drugging the nerves with morphia, neither have you cured by merely suggesting health or strength, unless the false mode of thinking or the immoral tendencies have first been replaced by true concepts and normal states. The desire for drink, or some other hidden cause, underlies the drink habit and it is the desire which must be eradicated and replaced by worthy motives before the habit is really overcome. Suggestion is the means of instituting changes in the mind in accordance with the truth. If I suggest to you, for instance, that instead of a material being having a "soul" you are a spiritual being clothed with a body, it is not merely the suggestion which may influence you, but much more the fundamental truth suggested which is potent once it gains ingress to your mind. Truth is the elixir of the mind and false belief its poison. To admit truth to the mind is like admitting sunlight to a room.

CHAPTER XII

AUTO-SUGGESTION 

AS one mind may impress another through suggestion, so may the individual suggest to himself the truth he desires to embody. He may suggest to his subconscious mind that physiological processes are normal, that nature through the subconscious is doing her work perfectly, aided by truth from the higher centres (instead of being interfered with as is the case when the mind entertains false beliefs and negative emotion) and this suggestion will not be without effect. He may suggest again to the higher level—the intellect—philosophic truth, until it becomes dominated by true concepts, and this is to gradually admit light to the dark chambers of his own mind.

This is practical auto-suggestion and it will be evident at once that its value depends on the kind and quality of the thought suggested. The solution of a problem in mathematics depends upon a knowledge of the principles of mathematics, and to satisfactorily avail ourselves of the use of auto suggestion we must have an understanding of the principles of Truth itself. Auto-suggestion is the means open to every mind to improve its own estate, to establish harmony within itself, to perfect its conscious relations with God and man and nature, and to foster and sustain normal conditions in its garment the body. It is therefore the means of self-help advocated in this book, and what has been said on practical psychology is but a preparation for the wise use of auto-suggestion, while the principles laid down in the preliminary chapters serve as the basis of its employment. Part III will consist merely in a general and practical application to life—that is to actual living—of what has already been said.

The value and uses of suggestion have been so thoroughly implied in the preceding pages that it will only be necessary to remind ourselves of the relation of thought to the brain and the nervous system, and of mental states and mental pictures to nervous reactions. It should be recognised, however, in regard to auto-suggestion, as with suggestion, that it may be of an undesirable as well as of a desirable character, and we are, in fact, unwittingly suggesting to ourselves all manner of things, good, bad, and indifferent. Thus we suggest that we are tired or ill, that we are moody or unhappy, or that our relations to people are inharmonious or selfish. The practical application of auto-suggestion means not only that we suggest desirable states of mind, but that we inhibit all contrary ideas and aim to form the habit of suggesting only that which has a basis in truth and conduces to harmony, serenity, and peace.

Any idea persistently dwelt upon, tends to occupy the field of consciousness to the exclusion of other thoughts. The monomaniac is thus the victim of self-hypnosis. The attention becomes absorbed in one idea which holds the mind spellbound. Obviously the remedy lies in distributing the attention among a number of wholesome ideas, and thus breaking the spell. One of the commonest forms of self-hypnosis is egotism. The egotist is chained to the central thought of himself, and, like a cow tied to a tree, as he goes round and round this centre, his rope grows shorter, his circle smaller, until at length he finds himself held rigidly against it. Another dominant idea with which man is prone to hypnotise himself is fear The fearful state easily becomes chronic and the subjection of the mind to fear is as literally hypnosis as is the subjection to the will of another. Let him who boasts his superiority to hypnotism, observe to what extent he may be self-hypnotised by dominant negative ideas and by his prejudices. Chronic invalids frequently have the habit of suggesting negative ideas to themselves which not only depress mental states but seriously interfere with physiological processes. Invalidism is with some merely a habit, the result of habitual negative auto-suggestion and the hypnosis of selfishness;—with some, but by no means with all, for there are many whose cheerfulness and unselfishness is an example worth following. It may happen, however, that the latter are self-hypnotised by the idea of resignation and are resigned to conditions which, did they but know it, are of their own making and could be overcome by mental effort in the right direction.

With this glance at the unfavourable side of auto-suggestion, let us now consider its beneficial aspects and its practical value. The fact is we are constantly indulging in auto-suggestion, therefore let us use it wisely and to our advantage and refrain from using it to our disadvantage. To centre the attention much upon oneself is a mistake and is likely to have a similar result to pressing the finger in the eye. Consciousness should rest on the body as little as possible, for it functions more normally under the subconscious alone than under the anxious supervision of consciousness. When it is advisable, however, to focus the mind upon oneself, let it be done systematically and in accordance with principle, precisely as one would attempt the solution of a problem by the rules of mathematics. Auto-suggestion is only truly efficient when it is thus systematic and the thought is concentrated. Let the idea which you wish to impress be brought to a focus through your mind, as rays of light are concentrated by a burning-glass. This is concentration and it is simple enough, requiring only constant practice. To distracted people, unaccustomed to concentrate their attention upon anything, it may seem very difficult, but all that is necessary in any case is practice, and the more it is practised the easier it becomes. It is good mental discipline and regarded merely in this light is worth while, for it strengthens and refreshes the mind.

Choose a favourable time and place, assume a comfortable position wherein the body makes no demand upon consciousness, and breathe deeply and regularly. Exclude all thoughts not bearing upon the subject and subdue the mind with firmness and patience until you have it well in hand, as you would hold in a horse and keep him to a steady gait. When you have brought the field of consciousness to the desired condition, frame for yourself a statement of the truth you wish to impress, as clearly, concisely, and forcibly as possible.

The nature of the suggestion will depend of course upon the particular truth it is desirable to bring into realisation. In general bear in mind that the Soul—which we may designate the real man—is itself wisdom, love, power, health, inasmuch as it is one with God the Source of all life and intelligence, and that it is only the stream of consciousness—the personal self—which is conditioned by illusions and false concepts. You are to purify this stream of consciousness by suggesting—pouring in, as it were—thoughts of absolute truth. Truth and error with reference to a given subject can no more occupy the mind at the same time than light and darkness can fill a room.

Consider the nature of man: first the self-as-knower—the Soul—deathless, diseaseless, free, and pure; the self-as-known, the stream of consciousness and its submerged depths—for ever changing; lastly the body, an outer garment built from within and picturing the dominant state of the mind. When the thoughts and feelings of this personal self are maintained in perfect harmony with the Soul, then is consciousness dominated by absolute truth which manifests itself in the body as health. This is harmony—to realise the Soul in consciousness, to be conscious of God, that is to say, Good, alone. Only in consciousness are we separated from God and this separation occurs whenever we think thoughts other than good. Love and good are real, like light; evil and error are unreal like darkness, are merely the absence of light. Consciously fill your mind with light, therefore, and it cannot be dark; fill it with harmony and it cannot be discordant; dwell upon reality and illusion will disappear from consciousness.

A truth held in mind will gradually penetrate the subconscious, and once fixed in subconsciousness will continue to react, in turn, upon consciousness. The submerged part of the average mind, normally in accord with Nature, has been vitiated by ignorant and ill-controlled thinking until it has become infected with fear, selfishness, and discord. If you wish to strengthen your muscles you take up systematic exercise, and similarly if you wish to invigorate and renew the mind you must devote yourself to the spiritual exercise of right-thinking.

As to specific suggestions, impress upon the mind always that which is desirable, that which you wish to bring into realisation for your true welfare. To dwell upon the undesirable state is to foster and perpetuate it. Remember, in this connection, that the individual consciousness is but an inlet to a larger stream, that the strength or power are derived from a universal source. Therefore do not limit yourself in consciousness and thus close the inlet, but make greater demands and open the doors wide, that energy may flow into you. The chances are you have limited yourself in every direction by your thoughts; now reverse the order of thought and work for your salvation—for this is the true salvation and the rational method of achieving it. Affirm love in place of fear, strength instead of weakness, courage instead of despondency, wisdom in place of ignorance; good and not evil, health, not disease; affirm and lose no opportunity of bringing it into manifestation by acting in harmony with your affirmation. This, in brief, is the rationale of auto-suggestion, the scientific means of self-help available to all.

CHAPTER XIII

FAITH

IT may not be generally recognised that faith has any basis in psychology, but such is the fact, for faith is merely a form of thought-energy in which the will is active under the stimulus of suggestion.

Faith is effective—faith in anything, even in nonsense; how much more potent, then, faith in truth, in principle. Faith in relics has cured many, but mark that the relic can do nothing, it is the *faith* itself in such instances which does all. Faith in a pill may be responsible for what the pill is supposed to do. Bread pills and coloured water have not infrequently been administered by physicians with excellent results. The patient under the belief that he is taking a powerful remedy, and with the assurance that it will produce good results, immediately pins his faith on the supposed medicine and it accomplishes the work. Faith in the doctor, himself, is remedial, and if any are skeptical of this we have Dr. Ostler's authority for the statement that faith is a large part of the doctor's stock in trade. It is little understood to what extent so-called remedies and various methods, are merely pegs to hang our faith on, and how often the faith rather than the object of faith is the active agent.

Faith requires an object upon which to focus itself and the nature of the object will depend upon the intelligence of the individual. As the intellect develops we constantly transfer our dependence from one set of objects or influences to another set. We laugh at the remedies our grandfathers believed in and our grandchildren will doubtless laugh at us. Educate a peasant and his faith in bones and bits of wood is gone and is perhaps replaced by belief in a Latin prescription—but one is little better than the other. Relics have been responsible, perhaps, for the more remarkable cures. To an intelligent man, however, the relic is of no use, for he can have no faith in it.

What then is the psychology of faith? Simply this, that faith in anything induces auto-suggestion. If you believe that something will help you, you constantly suggest this idea to yourself, you endow it with seeming power, the power meanwhile being resident in your own mind. You, therefore, unconsciously set your own forces to work, and the more active the faith, the more power do you unlock, arousing emotion, forming mental pictures, and of necessity inducing nervous reactions which may be of a wholly beneficial order. You may not consciously suggest to yourself but you set the subconscious to work. To borrow a phrase, you electrify or magnetise the subconscious by your objective faith, as you might magnetise an iron core by passing a current through the surrounding coil. Once faith is aroused, the subconscious becomes active.

The trouble is, we have so little faith in ourselves, while we are so ready to have faith in anything that is suggested to us with sufficient plausibility. Yet in most cases it is our own latent powers which are unlocked and which work for good or ill according to their direction. Quite as much as any fact in psychology this admonishes man to be his own friend, to foster his talent power and rely upon it, and have faith in that, rather than in the mere objects which inadvertently serve to unlock that power.

Self-trust is thus a sustaining force, and lack of it may defeat the ends to be attained. To have faith in yourself is to be your own friend; to be faithless to yourself is to be your own foe. Faith should be the accompaniment of all thought directed towards definite ends, for it of necessity gives added power—the power of conscious and subconscious suggestion. Such a mental state, where the will, directed towards the accomplishment of a purpose, is accompanied by faith in the ability to accomplish that result, is true prayer—the only kind of prayer, at any rate, which has any basis in practical psychology. "According to your faith be it unto you"—and there appear to be good grounds for the saying.

While faith is often inconsistent with reason, it should be borne in mind that faith is a mental force in itself and the object of faith merely serves to evoke that power. In this respect a relic which may serve with an ignorant peasant, or an incantation which may answer with a savage, will of course fail utterly with an educated man. The more one pursues science and philosophy, the less faith will he have in those things which appeal to the ignorant; and so it sometimes happens that highly trained scientific minds have very little faith left in anything. This is not unnatural in the course of mental evolution, but at the same time, it is an unfortunate state of mind to be in. Man cannot live and work to advantage without faith, and the growing philosopher, having discovered the nature of those things which attract and hold the ignorant and the thoughtless, should make haste to establish his faith on philosophic and reasonable grounds. Let him put his faith in that alone which is unchangeable, namely in God, the source of all life, intelligence, power; upon Truth which is the same to-day, to-morrow, and forever, and upon his own essential Self which is one with God, unconditioned and immutable, while the shifting stream of consciousness changes with its varying beliefs.

It will be readily seen that faith in eternal Principle and in oneself as the normal instrument of divine activities is a large factor in the philosophy of self-help. Hold fast to your faith then, but transfer it, from objective uncertainties and the creations of the imagination, to subjective realities. You have lost faith in bones and relics, in the anthropomorphic God of theology, and sooner or later you must lose faith in drugs. Establish your faith now in the true God who is Spirit and dwell in the normal consciousness that the self-as-knower, the Soul, is one with God and hence likewise unconditioned.

It is wisdom, freedom, and purity as God is wisdom, freedom, and purity. All mutations are in the stream of consciousness, and in the body which reflects its changes. Aim ever to maintain your consciousness in harmony with the Soul, and whenever the mind wanders from truth, as wander it will, bring it back by means of auto-suggestion to those eternal principles by which God finds expression in us. Do this in the abiding faith that those principles are sufficient for all the needs of human life and activity and that man's departure from them through ignorance or perversion is the one cause of his troubles. Have faith that the truth will make you free and in truth take your refuge.

PART III

PHILOSOPHY OF LIFE

CHAPTER I

CHARACTER

WE may now inquire as to what philosophy of life is to be deduced from the foregoing facts of psychology and what effect a recognition of these facts and principles may be expected to produce upon character and upon health. Such a recognition must influence at once the nature of our views and lead us to substitute, to the best of our ability, controlled for uncontrolled thinking, true in place of false concepts. It will, in short, imbue us with the dominant idea of self-control, that is to say, control and direction of the thought-force; for it can hardly fail to reveal more clearly the nature of cause and effect and our own responsibility in the matter. Much that we have heretofore assumed to be altogether independent of ourselves, much that we have laid at the door of "bad luck" or attributed to the inscrutable acts of Providence, will now appear in its true light as merely the objective effect of a subjective cause for which we ourselves are responsible. If it has been our habit to defend ourselves with the excuse that, as we did not know that two and two made four we were not to blame for our miscalculations, we must now admit that it is our business to know it, and that we cannot too soon acquaint ourselves with the fact, that in future our calculation may be correct. If again we have been inclined to blame others for our troubles, we must now admit that, while this may occasionally be justified, it is not the rule but the exception, and that ignorance and fear are our real enemies; that we have stood in our own light and created most of our own troubles.

A recognition of the simple fact alone that all consciousness is motor cannot fail to have a considerable influence. But the realisation of the deeper fact that, as there are principles of mathematics, so there are principles of Truth absolute, which underly our relation to God and to man, and that failure to comply with these in our attitude to life must manifest itself in both mental and physical inharmony, inasmuch as health is harmony and harmony is conformity to principle—such a realisation is the most practical awakening which can come to the mind. What is the basic fact of our philosophy? It is this: that the self-as-knower—the Soul—is one with God, the universal knower, the subject of knowledge; whereas the self-as-known, the stream of consciousness, is the agent, subject to development and control, and the body merely its garment or material envelope. This means that God is immanent in us, that we may appropriate the divine energy in the measure of our capacity to realise it in consciousness and give it expression in our lives.

Man is a spiritual being clothed with a body, and a character fashioned upon this basis is necessarily both superior to and more stable than one fashioned after the false postulate that man is a material being and that he may or may not have a "soul."

Mind is the potter and matter the clay and not only was the potter destined to mould the clay according to his will, but to conform his will to the divine Will which is wisdom. The implication is not alone the ultimate triumph of mind over matter but the victory of the higher over the lower in consciousness, of positive over negative states of mind, of love over fear and selfishness, of wisdom over ignorance. Our evolution is in consciousness alone and is reflected in matter. The Soul with God stands firm. (It is never that which we know but always that *by* which we are able to know.) Our salvation is evolution towards the light, an uncovering of the Soul; salvation is in wisdom alone.

No one grows wise by another's thinking and surely there is no clearer indication of character than the persistent effort to think for oneself. For this purpose our minds, the higher centres at least, were provided us—that we should do our own thinking. Only weak minds will be satisfied with ready-made thought as only weak stomachs can sustain themselves on predigested food. The most profound influence of our philosophy upon character will be an awakening to the necessity of using our minds instead of allowing them to be used by stronger mentalities. It shall lead one to ask himself—"Do I think, or do others think for me? Am I really the agent of my acts, or am I the puppet of religious dogmas, medical superstitions, and of race beliefs?" This attitude of intellectual self-reliance will lead one to speedily dismiss some false beliefs long entertained because never examined, beliefs with reference to God and to the nature of man himself. Furthermore, those true precepts which may have been instilled in his mind by parents and teachers, he shall now make his own for the first time and thus truly incorporate them in his moral life by giving them the sanction of his own reason.

If this intellectual self-reliance and this recognition of cause and effect in our mental life implies added responsibility, it also insures an increased sense of power. As we are said commonly to use but one sixth of our lung capacity in breathing, so we avail ourselves of but a small fraction of that power which is latent in us. The natural result of a better understanding of oneself is the desire to utilise the power revealed and to overcome the obstacles which may prevent, and this is to work for the efficiency and perfection of character. Self-reliance is the basis of character and many a man, be it said, who is esteemed strong and wise is merely depending upon the strength of others and would fall if his crutch were removed. Always we work out our own salvation. We acquire mental power by thinking for ourselves, as we gain muscular strength by the exercise of our muscles—not by reading about exercise. Only that truth which we have made our own sustains us in time of need.

When we have perceived the right road, we must also have the will to follow or our perception is of little practical value. Psychology has shown us how desirable it is to be our own friends in a very literal sense—to control our thoughts, to establish wholesome and friendly habits, and to make the nervous system an ally. The agent in accomplishing this is the will, and character has been defined as "a completely fashioned will," but *self-control*, in the light of the clearer understanding of the relation of mind and body which psychology makes possible, has received an added significance. It means not a superficial control alone but a control and direction of the thought-force itself; it means the promotion of sane and healthful thinking and the inhibition of unwholesome thoughts and emotions. Right-thinking becomes the dominant motive of the balanced and spiritual mind. It not only precedes right conduct but it also precedes healthy nervous reactions.

Now right-thinking is based on truth and sincerity. It rests on no such flimsy foundation as religious cant, philosophic pretension, or mere cleverness. The heart must be right or all else is vain. The love of truth, the love of righteousness, the love of one's fellows, are the elements of true character. We have no new doctrine of ethics to expound but our psychology throws a new light on the subject. We must not only do good, we must *think* good; we must think of others as we would have them think of us—and better. Good must rule the mind; we must ally ourselves with the good wherever found, and with the good alone. Love is the normal attitude to God and to mankind. The more we love the more Godlike we are, for God is Love and Love is life. To exclude love from consciousness, to live a loveless existence, is to separate oneself in mind from God—to dwarf and stultify oneself. While character may be defined as a completely fashioned will, it is surely more: namely, a will fashioned in accordance with the good, the beautiful, and the true, a will which leads us to preserve the integrity of our minds by thinking in accordance with the dictates of wisdom.

The conception of the nature of man and his relation to God here entertained is, of course, that which should have the most profound influence upon character, for it is the fundamental postulate of spiritual philosophy

—the same philosophy which Jesus preached when he said:

"I and my Father are one."

"The Kingdom of Heaven is within."

"It is the spirit that quickeneth: the flesh profiteth nothing."

The body is an instrument merely, good in its place and normally an efficient servant of the spiritual master. It is neither to be pampered nor to be condemned, but to be kept in its place and made to perform its true functions. The body is not the man nor is sensation life; this is merely the point of view of the unregenerate man, from which happily he may be reborn into the realisation of man as spirit and life as righteousness and peace.

Character is always acquired. It is true some are better born than others, but in any case it is a question of what we do with our talent. Of those who have much, much is expected. The main purpose of this book is to reveal to you, whoever you are and whatever your circumstances, how great is the latent power within you, if you will develop it; how great is the supply if you will avail yourself.

God is the Source of your life, your will,

your intelligence. The philosophy of life, the secret of strength, is to bring God into your life and consciousness. The highest self-reliance is reliance upon the Soul which is God in us. To bring God into consciousness means to lead a clean and upright life and to persistently dwell upon love and truth, —to establish the normal habit of right-thinking.

CHAPTER II

IDEALS

CHARACTER is formed by the will in accordance with the ideals we hold in mind. Putting aside all mediæval dogmas of future reward and punishment, let us remember that heaven or harmony is within and is virtually a state of mind—a consciousness, that is, which is normal in its attitude to the several relations of life, which is freed from false beliefs and dominated by true concepts. Every hour is the hour of judgment, for cause and effect, like gravity, are always operative All is in accordance with Law. As a man thinketh so is he. It is impossible, therefore, that we should think falsely and at the same time express harmony in our lives. Happiness is an effect of which right-thinking is the cause. It lies only in the direction which wisdom indicates. Obviously it is impossible to follow a wrong road and reach the goal. Yet this is precisely what men try to do in the world and their lives end in disappointment at not reaching that destination which lay in the very opposite direction.

Chief among these false roads, which lead to the destruction of our hopes at least, is the highway of selfishness. Since happiness does not lie in this direction it is of little consequence how well we proceed on the road; we are going the wrong way and every step takes us further from the goal. Selfishness is based on a wrong ideal of life, the idea of acquiring and achieving at the expense of others, an idea as false as it is unprofitable, yet which underlies the commercial and to a large extent the social life to-day. The whole force of the world-thought tends to impress this false ideal upon the individual mind, and the money-mad shove and jostle one another on the road which leads to despair.

A second highway is the road of the senses, and this leads not to happiness but to disease. This road is followed under the false idea that sensation is life, that pleasure is happiness, and that eating and drinking are ends in themselves. Alas, how bitter is the awakening. The merry Eaters and Drinkers of to-day are the hollow-eyed spectres of to-morrow. Pleasure ends not in happiness, but in pain. The tyranny of the senses means the gradual atrophy of the higher spiritual sense, the loss of the perception of values and of aspiration and nobility. It is a levelling downward, a burrowing into the earth until little by little the light is shut out.

Of false ideals—of wrong roads—there is no end. And the point is, that they are not snares to entrap the unwary, planned by some enemy of the world, but merely paths beaten by the feet of mankind in its errant search for happiness, and into which each succeeding generation heedlessly wanders. If you are weary of following the wrong road you can retrace your steps. If you have discovered the right road, lose no time in following it, for in that direction alone is happiness. Remember that few if any have been born with their feet on the true path. Those who have found it have usually done so after many efforts in the wrong direction. Take heart then. He is twice a man who is neither led nor driven, but, having suffered in the wilderness of his ignorance, turns at length to the light and of his own accord follows the true way.

We are but grown-up children, and like children we learn by experience that certain ways are profitable and others to be avoided. Experience and philosophy are two roads to the same point. Experience is the long road of the ignorant; philosophy the short cut of the wise. A child does not reason about the fire, but burns himself and thenceforth avoids it. It is not necessary that we should always burn ourselves in order to discover the facts, for if we will but use our reasoning powers, we may often come directly at the truth without the intervening experience. As a rule, however, we listen too much to the world and give no heed to the inner voice. We are hypnotised by the world-thought, carried away in the tumultuous stream of consciousness and tossed in the rapids of false beliefs. Learn to still the mind, that truth may make itself known through the admonitions of the Soul; for the Soul is not subject to experience: it is God in us, God who is absolute Love and Truth.

To hold true ideals in mind is, to that extent, to be one in consciousness with truth—to bridge the gulf which exists in consciousness alone between God and the individual. This is the philosophic at-one-ment which means harmony, and the result of such harmony must be, not only peace of mind but nervous reactions conducive to health. Let us bear in mind always that health is harmony and the efficient means of its realisation is by the impression of true ideals through auto-suggestion; as the means of solving a problem in mathematics is to bring to mind the principles and apply them. The ideal state, of course, would be habitual right-thinking, the habit of always reacting upon true ideals. Obviously no lifetime is long enough for such perfection. But no matter how distant the goal, the first and chief consideration is—are we travelling in the right direction?

To meditate upon true ideals, to clearly frame them in mind and concentrate the thought upon them to the exclusion of all else, is literally to sow the seed—and God will give the increase. As we sow we shall reap. No one has ever gathered figs from thistles. If you have been sowing thistles in your mind—thoughts of fear or selfishness, of weakness or disease—do not cry out against Fate when your crop matures. Do nothing further to foster the growth of the weeds. Let your weed patch die for lack of recognition and meanwhile do you cultivate new fields and plant this time good seed.

If we have been all our lives sowing thistles we cannot expect in a day to reverse this order. But if any one will sow seeds of love and truth, and foster them with the same care and energy he has devoted to thoughts of fear and of error, he shall be repaid and shall reap a hundred-fold.

Nature works always for health. The moral force of the universe is drawing man towards God, that is towards the absolute Good. Pain and disease and much of our trial and tribulation result from the obstruction we offer in consciousness to the flow of the divine current. In our ignorance, in place of going with the current by shaping our lives in accordance with love and truth, we vainly essay to resist and go against the current. The Law is never broken, but we are broken upon it. If a sculptor wishes to model a perfect form, he studies and keeps before him a perfect model, not a distorted one, and by concentrating his attention and his energy upon an ideal, he is able to give it corresponding expression in his work. Were he to hold fixedly in mind the image of a cripple, it would be impossible for him at the same time to model a perfect figure. Similarly if the mind is to manifest harmony within itself and in the body, it must be centred upon true ideals and must give no room to distorted, crippled, or diseased thoughts. By dwelling upon true ideals we give free course to Truth to become operative in us; we admit spiritual light to the mind and in that light the dormant seeds of righteousness, peace, and harmony germinate and develop. Truth is to the spiritual world what light is to the vegetable world. False beliefs are literally a barrier to the spiritual light. By our own ignorance we veil the mind and keep ourselves in the dusk of illusion, where, like plants in a cellar, we can manifest only a feeble life.

Take the plant out of the cellar and place it in the sunlight and it grows in virtue of the life-force and the action of the sun. To lift your thoughts out of the cellar of your being and bring them into the air and sunshine, by dwelling upon true ideals of life, is to place yourself in the normal environment where Truth works her own way in you. The plant grows only in virtue of the life-force which is cosmic, and yet by merely withholding the light we may annul the influence of a cosmic force as far as it applies to that particular plant. Just so, man is destined for certain spiritual conditions, his outer life being merely a reflex of his inner adaptation to the normal ideal. By merely opposing the flimsy barrier of ignorance, therefore, to the spiritual light of Truth, he throws himself out of his normal relation to life and thrives no better than a plant denied the sunlight.

The fundamental ideals which are, as it were, the inlets of absolute Truth into the individual consciousness, are implied in those facts of metaphysics, ethics, and psychology which we have been considering. The ethical ideas in particular are familiar to us. But we have yet to learn how far our departure from those ideals in thought is responsible for our failure to maintain both mental harmony and health. Systematic auto-suggestion of truth to the mind is the efficient means, however, of regulating the disordered consciousness and of finally establishing that state of harmony which is normal to the spiritual life.

CHAPTER III

THE INNER LIFE

OUR study of the nature of man and his relation to God has shown us that his real life is in spirit. Our experience with the world, on the other hand, reveals how little he lives this true life and how exclusively his interest is absorbed in a material and wholly objective life. More than this, the experience of most men proves to them, sooner or later, how unprofitable is this objective life if lived to itself alone. Men do not commonly consider, however, how intimately their philosophy of life is related to their prevailing mental states and thus to their health as well. All the cynical old men say we can gather no figs in this life. They do not take into account that they have sown only thistles.

If you sow only to the senses, you shall reap the fruit of the senses, which is Pain; and if you sow to the material you shall reap the fruit of the material, which is Weariness.

Man born of woman is of few days and full of trouble, but man born of the Spirit is of eternity. If you worship Mammon you shall receive the reward of Mammon, which is despair, and if you worship God you shall receive the reward of God, which is peace. Choose, then, whom you will serve. Rest assured, not in this world or the next is there any departure from the natural sequence of cause and effect.

It is true that since we have bodies we must have a relation to the material world. But we should establish a normal relation. The body is good, money is good, food is good; but when we become absorbed in eating and drinking, or in acquiring money, or in the care of the body, to the exclusion of our true and spiritual aims—then, and only then, these things are bad. One and all are means, never an end in life, and when we falsely elevate them in consciousness to a ruling place, they invariably become tyrants.

The body has no health or strength in itself. It has no life apart from the informing mind. If that consciousness be in harmony with truth then will the body show forth harmony, and if that consciousness be discordant the body must manifest discord, as a mirror reflects an object. Now the inner life is a consecration to the Spirit, an effort to establish and maintain a consciousness in harmony with God, that is to say, with love and truth. Love casteth out fear and the truth makes free, therefore in these should we take refuge.

If we have prepared a place within, we may retire at will and find peace. But if we have cultivated only objective states of mind and placed our whole dependence in material things, where shall we turn? For these things must fail as they have failed a host of deluded men before us. Each one must prepare a sanctuary for himself, and in the measure that he has consecrated himself to the inner life and meditated upon the truth, he has made it his own and it will serve him in time of need.

In the journey of life, every traveller comes to the branching roads that lead to the Without and the Within. Every step on the road of the Without takes us further from the centre; the road of the Within leads to God. The true means of self-help, because it is the very purpose of life, is to find our centre, to bring our consciousness into harmony with God; for God is our life and our strength and apart from God we are nothing.

God is to man what the Sun is to the sunbeam, what the dynamo is to the individual light. Only as we live from within can we avail ourselves fully of the divine current of which the personal self is but the means of transmission. The spiritual laws of our being supply the conditions under which we shall best transmit that power. Every departure from these laws is a disturbance of those conditions, and to live from without is to receive and transmit only a fraction of the power which we should normally manifest in a spiritual life.

You may think because you attend all the lectures and have read the latest books that you are living from within. Do not deceive yourself. Silence and meditation are the means of following the way. Not reading about life but *living* avails. The most any one can do for you is to inspire you to think for yourself and to thus help yourself. Neither does attending church mean that you are living from within. Repeating dogmas by rote will help you no more than it helps the parrot who might be taught to do the same. If you believe salvation comes through the sacrifice and death of some one else—your brother, for instance, you are still in the pit of ignorance. Yet it is from ignorance alone that we need salvation, and ignorance is overcome by wisdom, as darkness is dispelled by light; not by another's wisdom but by our own. Only the truth we have *realised* profits us. If your idea of prayer is to petition God to change the order of things, so that water may run up hill, you are not on the road to salvation. You have no enemy but your own ignorance, and not until you have realised the truer ideal of God and a more spiritual conception of prayer can you advance.

Sentimental and theoretical religions merely blind us to the necessity of helping ourselves and promoting our own salvation through right-thinking and the realisation of the true self. Self-help comes through practical religion—the realisation of truth and the living in accordance with the dictates of wisdom. This is the inner life—not sanctimonious airs and prayers on the housetop, but a life of silent prayer, in which the controlling motive is the love of truth and righteousness and the effort to bring love and truth into expression. Right-thinking is the prayer of sanity; thoughts of kindness and considerateness the prayer of love; thoughts of wholeness the prayer of health.

In our busy objective life with its multitudinous cares and its almost complete absorption in things, no time is left for meditation. Hence the universal dissatisfaction and unrest, for man can not possibly live by bread alone. The spiritual man is not properly nourished, for the attention is centred wholly upon the physical man and his wants, or at least upon the intellectual man. This slow starving of the spiritual nature is responsible for the paucity and barrenness of our lives. Do you not see that the spiritual is necessarily the foundation, the rock upon which the superstructure of life, both intellectual and physical, should rest? You who are seeking a light in the darkness, hasten to establish yourself at the centre. Lay the solid spiritual foundation of a new and better life. Seek first the Kingdom of God which is righteousness and peace. It is impossible to rear a perfect structure upon a foundation of fear, of ignorance, or of selfishness.

In right-thinking we conserve the interests of the whole man, for we thus maintain both body and mind efficient instruments of higher activities. Man is a stream of which God is the Source. It is by right-thinking and medi tation upon true ideals that he shall keep himself open to that Source, and as he does this he shall have life more abundantly.

Learn to retire in the silence and devote some time each day to meditation and concentration upon practical truths, that you may renew and strengthen yourself. Refresh the mind in this manner as you refresh the body by the morning tub. Our strength lies in the realisation of God in us; our weakness in the apparent separation which is our delusion. In silence alone, in that inner sanctuary which we have prepared, we shall come to this deeper realisation. Learn to still the mind and to shut out the turbulent thoughts of the world, the desires and fears and confusion. Only when the surface of the water is perfectly still does it reflect the heavens. The disturbed consciousness receives no intimations from within. The din and clamour of our own thoughts may deafen us to truth. Inhibit therefore; come to rest! Be still and let truth be reflected in your mind. Thus is acquired that which is superior to an intellectual, namely a spiritual relf-reliance. It is thus the foundation of life is laid upon a rock. But the life, the strength, and the wisdom are of God, and the highest self-reliance is God-reliance. In the light of this fact the sonorous verses of the Psalmist have a real and practical significance:

"The Lord is my light and my salvation; whom shall I fear? The Lord is the strength of my life; of whom shall I be afraid?"

"For in the time of trouble he shall hide me in his pavilion: in the secret of his tabernacle shall he hide me; he shall set me up upon a rock."

"Wait on the Lord: be of good courage, and he shall strengthen thine heart; wait, I say, on the Lord."

CHAPTER IV

POISE

THE application of our practical philosophy and psychology has resulted, let us hope, in a somewhat different attitude to the external world and in a new measure of self-control; in a greater intellectual and moral self-reliance; and lastly in a deeper spiritual self-reliance, a nearer approach to God, through the recognition that the Soul—the self-as-knower—is God in us. The fruits, that is, are poise, freedom, and power in some increased measure, and, as a result, a more stable health. The price of liberty, be it said, is eternal vigilance. It has been suggested that we entrust this vigilance as much as possible to the subconscious by forming *habits* of right-thinking with corresponding reactions, and thus relieve ourselves of the burden of a too conscious supervision.

Poise is the direct result of self-control; but an efficient self-control is more than mere willing in itself, like that of the stoical savage, for it has good grounds in both philosophy and psychology. Sensation, as we have seen, is a mental state induced by external vibrations. We may not be able to control the vibrations; we may not be able to control the sensation to which they give rise—though this can be done to some extent; what we can control is our attitude to the sensation and our opinion about it. It is only common sense, then, that we should devote our energy to regulating that which is susceptible of regulation, while we waste no time or energy on that which can not be controlled. Here is the ideal philosophic state. With the uncontrolled mind the case is quite the opposite. The weather may be inclement but, as we can not change the weather, the reasonable thing is to lay all stress upon our attitude to it. It is possible to change that so as to adapt ourselves to external conditions. The noise in the street may be annoying. If it can not be silenced, let the mental attitude be so regulated that the noise ceases to be annoying or is even no longer heard. To control the mental state, rather than to uselessly disturb oneself over external conditions which can not be controlled, is a sound philosophic theory capable of endless applications in daily life—and of no value unless it *is* applied. We all have our peculiarities and our susceptibilities. Some are sensitive to one thing, some to another. To be hypersensitive to a great many things means the gradual breaking down of the nervous system, unless self-control is established.

It is never so much the thing or condition as our attitude to it, which counts. The old Stoics wisely laid great stress on not enlarging upon the reports of our senses. If we are in danger of drowning we forget that a few quarts are sufficient and imagine we are to swallow the ocean. The imagination, like a newspaper reporter, exaggerates the simplest fact and garbles the news which the senses bring in. Thus we sit and tremble at the creations of the imagination. We are disturbed far more by our opinions of a thing than by the thing itself.

It is very evident we have it in our power to govern our opinions, to check the tendency of the imagination to exaggeration, and to maintain a normal mental attitude under many circumstances where we are too apt to be controlled rather than to control. If we can not govern sensation, we can at least govern the attitude towards it. But can we never hope to govern sensation itself? There is reason to think we may to some extent. If hypnotism has done nothing else, it has at least thrown a new light upon sensation and shown how relative is its nature. In the hypnotic state bitter tastes sweet, heat is cold, and pain is pleasure, at the will of the hypnotiser. A blister is raised on the hand by merely suggesting it, it is painful or not in accordance with the suggestion, it disappears at the time suggested. Sensation is thus shown to be more or less relative to the whole mental state of which it is a phase. When it fails to excite the attention, it practically does not exist to consciousness. You may be so absorbed as not to hear a bell or not to see what is taking place directly in front of you. Instances are cited of soldiers who, in the excitement of battle, were not aware they had been shot. The implication in all this is that we may so learn to govern the mind as to be less sensitive to pain, as by the cultivation of the æsthetic we certainly become more sensitive to impressions of beauty.

The mind may be compared to a glass through which we look; therefore attend to the glass. The cloud which you think you see in the sky, may be merely a flaw in the lens through which you make your observation. If life appears dark, clean your glass and look again. It will appear brighter now. If another's character seems somewhat distorted, observe first if your glass be not out of focus. We are often enough disturbed by apparent conditions, which are in reality merely flaws in our glass. The secret of poise is to keep the mental glass clean and in focus, and many disturbing elements in life are thus eliminated, for they have no existence other than in our own minds.

Poise is first an inner adjustment always. If we are not in harmony within ourselves we can not be in harmony with life. Our worst foes are they of our own household. Yet almost invariably the blame is laid at some one else's door. To be harmonious within ourselves means to have made friends of will, habit, and imagination, to have made an ally of the nervous system, and to have established a normal attitude to the various relations of life.

As before remarked, we are attentive to that in which we are interested, or that which we fear. When we remove fear we become less attentive to the details which give rise to it. Thus as our interest is more centred in the things of the spirit and we come to live the inner life, we are less attentive to and therefore less disturbed by outer conditions. The outer world is by nature impermanent. Without, all is change. Hence as long as we live to the material we can not but be moved by its mutations. If we are to stand firm, we must have our feet on firm ground. Only that mind which has found its centre, remains serene when the troubled winds of the world blow over it, and being serene, it reflects the heavens of the inner life, the infinite repose of the Soul.

The details of self-control and the regulation of consciousness are merely practical psychological adjustments, but underlying true serenity is the religious life and faith in the unchangeable God immanent in us. If you believe God to be subject to change at your whim, where will you find any solid ground in the whole universe? If you have put your faith in the worldly life, how can you have any peace, for it is a light that fails, and you must soon depart in any event? If you have not opened your mind to truth, then you are a prey to the false beliefs of the world-thought, to all its fears and superstitions, and to the mental disturbance and disease which accompany them.

Truth alone satisfies. Only in the spiritual life has man ever found peace. This is a practical book and we are dealing with practical things. If the inner life were not a practical life for to-day, its consideration would have no place here. The Soul alone is enduring and hence real in a metaphysical sense. The spiritual life is that alone which is eternal and hence real and practical in a philosophic sense. A machine, nothing in itself, is merely an arrangement to bring energy into play. It is of value only as it fulfils its purpose. So the personal self is an instrument merely to bring the Spirit into manifestation. The machine has no energy of itself but energy is brought into use through it. The same may be said of man. He must be properly adjusted and well-regulated in accordance with the laws of his being in order that the divine current may flow through him. The mechanism of his mind and body are of value only as they perform their office. Unlike a machine, he has self-consciousness and he may become so absorbed in the wheels and cogs of his mechanism that he is oblivious to the purpose for which they are designed.

The real man is not a wheel nor a cog but is one with the energy which uses wheels and cogs, and the conditions under which the human mechanism does its best work are trust and serenity.

CHAPTER V

FREEDOM

ONE who has recognised the principles upon which the philosophy of self-help is based, to say nothing of the exceedingly practical relation of psychology to living, can hardly fail to have as a result a new conception, if not a new sense, of freedom. It will have occurred to him that the most prevalent form of slavery is a bondage to false beliefs and to the tyranny of the senses, and that this concerns him more nearly than any Social or Political tyranny whatsoever. He will have concluded, therefore, that true freedom lies in the perception of truth and in perfect self-control, and that, as he has been in slaverv to his own sensations and opinions, he may now be his own liberator.

As ignorance binds, truth makes us free. Every false belief is a link in the chain; but wisdom overcomes ignorance, as love casts out fear and light dispels darkness. Mental and moral evolution is, therefore, always in the direction of freedom. Defects of character and disposition are obstacles we interpose between ourselves and the light, obstacles to our own progress. As these are surmounted one by one, we see more clearly, and experience greater freedom. Enlightenment and freedom go hand in hand. False belief shackles us, for whatever we believe stands to us in the place of truth, and usurpers are never just rulers. The Astecs were vanquished more by their own fear and superstition than by any prowess of the Spaniards, and were thus enslaved because of beliefs which obscured their vision of the facts and paralysed their activity. In like manner we are all victims to our own fears and to false concepts, which shut out the light of truth and diminish our native energy, if they do not wholly obstruct our activity. Let us not blame either Society or Fate, then, for conditions which are personal to us and for which we have the remedy in our own hands.

While there is much discussion in regard to hypnotism, apparently no one has recognised the fact that we are all hypnotised, more or less, by the world-thought. As this is one of the factors which militates against our freedom, there is something to be said of the necessity for *de*hypnotisation. The important question is not—can we be hypnotised or no; but being already in a state of hypnosis, how are we to be dehypnotised and freed from the tyranny of false world-beliefs? Some are in the profound hypnotic sleep and their acts are purely automatic, their opinions wholly reflected. Others are merely in a drowsy state and are obedient only to the hypnosis of certain ideas from which they have never been free This hypnosis, begun by their parents, by stupid nurses and silly Sunday-school teachers, has been fostered ever since by the verbose nonsense of the newspapers and by the pressure of the world-thought itself.

There is only one remedy for ignorance and that is enlightenment, but if you do not know you are in slavery you will not seek freedom. The most hopeless class intellectually are the half-educated who think they are wise. And in this day of the general diffusion of cheap knowledge and half-truths, when every one has a smattering of information, and people learn from the newspapers a thousand things which are not true, this class is rapidly growing. Instead of thinking for themselves, as they fondly suppose, they are merely reflecting opinions and their point of view depends on the paper they take.

It is a hopeful sign when any man becomes intellectually self-reliant—a sign of developing character: when he accepts a theory, because on his own recognisance he believes it to be essentially good and not simply because others think so; when he essays to examine popular notions concerning ethics, religion, and hygiene and rejects or accepts them at his own disceretion. He is in a fair way to free himself from much superstition and false belief which cramps the mind and inhibits its power; he is on the road to intellectual freedom. Self-trust is inseparable from character, and to inspire any one to a greater degree of self-trust is above all to help him to help himself. If we do not think for ourselves—if we have the habit of delegating others to do our thinking for us—the fibre of the mind grows flabby like an unused muscle. If we are to run a race we must gradually strengthen the muscles and the lungs to that end. And if we are to work out our salvation we must so strengthen the mind by use that we are able to think for ourselves, to detect error from truth, and be able to withstand the pressure of the world-thought and the foolish opinions of our neighbours. It is only by thinking for ourselves, and the enlightenment which ensues, that we are enabled to awake from the hypnotic trance in which tradition, superstition, and false belief have held us.

There is much discussion, too, concerning the freedom of the will. So far as our destiny is cosmic we have no choice, inasmuch as we did not elect that there should be a Universe or that we should be an integral part of it. But in so far as we build our own characters, and by the quality of our thought invite the mental state and the nervous reactions which follow, we certainly have the freedom of the will.

"But," say the Fatalists, "you had to think that way because you are you, and therefore you are not responsible for what follows." Determinism is always the refuge of the weak and the self-indulgent and always will be. When we grow strong we renounce it. This specious argument, any one who has determined to be a man can refute for himself by the facts of his own life, if he will look squarely at them and attempt no evasion or self-apology. Let him answer, when he comes to a turn in the road, whether he has a choice or not, and if not—why? If the dipsomaniac *must* take a drink, is it a force without or within himself which so decrees? Why, it is the force of *habit* is it not, which has temporarily overcome his will? And this habit, you must admit, was of his own creation. What power it has, he himself gave it by persistent recognition and cultivation. We have always energy enough to form habits while life lasts. Let him cultivate some wholesome habits and as these grow they will withdraw the attention from the drink habit, while at the same time he stimulates the will by exercise, until the spell is broken. By continued lack of recognition, thenceforth, the habit will die, for habits are only kept alive by use. Power lies not in drink, nor in anything else external to us, but in the mental attitude we cultivate. It is our own force which we invoke and then turn against ourselves. To help another, then, is primarily to help him turn his force in the right direction and to further develop it. He may need help at the start—most of us have at one time or another; but once started in the right direction, his own force increases with cultivation, for the same reason that his bad habits developed with use.

Freedom is thus largely an adjustment of inner states to outer conditions. It is not so much the environment which counts as the manner in which we react upon that environment. What is your ability to interpose the will between the afferent impressions and the efferent result? Aim to increase that ability, for it makes for poise, for power, and for freedom. The ape is an afferent machine, and the man who obeys always the impression is a slave to the afferent. To act under the stimulus of will and of reason is the part of the free man. To act from afferent impression, from the tickling of the senses, is the part of the slave. Sensation is good if it serves, bad if it rules. But whether it rules or serves depends upon the efficiency of the will and also upon interest. For if the attention is centred upon the body it takes to itself some unction and makes increasing demands upon the attention. This is to speak figuratively, for it is in reality the mind, which reacts upon itself by being centred upon the body. There is no freedom for us so long as we are dominated by the senses or tyrannised over by the consciousness of the body. If such be the case, let us withdraw the attention from bodily conditions and distribute it among spiritual and intellectual considerations. It were better so in any case, for freedom is in that quarter —never in any other, and Freedom, like the muse, must be invited. She dwells only on the high places, and in the lower strata of consciousness she can not live.

As we cultivate an interest in spiritual things, in truth, and in beauty, the attention is provided the normal field upon which to focus itself. This is the value of resources— that they take us out of ourselves. The personality is like a mechanism devised for a certain work. To be self-centred is to be so absorbed in the machine as to entirely lose sight of the purpose for which it is designed, the work it is to do. Self-centred persons are always self-hypnotised. The mental currents stagnate within them. But to love the work, to be absorbed in the Purpose for which the personal instrument came into existence, is to keep the current circulating from within outward, to expand in the direction of freedom. We may cherish our whims and our self-love if we will, but we must remember they are links in the chain which binds. Only the wise and spiritually minded are free.

CHAPTER VI

POWER

AS an efficient regulation of the mental forces and the wise dominion of the will over attention, habit, and imagination, insures a greater degree of poise and some sense of freedom, it means at the same time an accession of power, not only through the regulation of our forces, but through the development of latent force.

Much of our distress in life is occasioned by misdirected energy, we ourselves having first developed the force through concentration of the will upon some habit, or whim, and thus turned it against ourselves. We liberate power but we waste it. Energy is at the same time withdrawn from legitimate channels and our proper activities suffer. The problem with man, as with the locomotive, is to render more energy available both by opening channels to it and by checking waste. In this sense, psychology does for us what mechanics does for the engine. Neither create energy—they merely aim to render it available by concentrating and controlling it.

There are points in any mechanism where power is always lost, as, for instance, in friction, and engineering is ever concerned with devising means for reducing the loss. Similarly there are points in the mental machinery where power escapes, even in a fairly well-regulated mind. Friction of any kind—mental inharmony, that is—is a source of great waste. Negative emotion, such as worry and fear, is a constant leak. Lack of concentration—a distracted attention—is another. Susceptibility to adverse suggestion also; to say nothing of lack of self-control and a nervous system that works not for, but against us.

What are the conditions then under which we best conserve power? Obviously those in which we have made our own faculties friendly to our best interest, so that one and all work for the general good: a disciplined and well-disposed household, in other words. This brings us back to the habit of right-thinking and the normal reactions which ensue, for only such a well-adjusted mechanism will develop full power. The use of auto-suggestion as an efficient means of impressing true ideals upon the mind and of perfecting this adjustment naturally suggests itself in this connection. Consciousness, unless it be serene, tends to obstruct normal subconscious processes and to throw mind and body out of adjustment. It is therefore absolutely necessary that we eliminate false beliefs and control our thinking if we are to express any freedom in life or to avail ourselves of our normal power.

If there is one fact more than another that should be emphasised with reference to the philosophy of self-help, it is that life is a whole in which the parts are related, and that what affects any part must affect the whole. Ethics, morals, health, are bound up together. Nothing is wholly detached or separate. Our home life, our attitude to our fellows, have the most intimate relation to health of mind and body. What we do for another, we do for ourselves; what we take from another, we take from ourselves as well. Every insincerity vitiates the home-life and if the home-life is not true and harmonious, character and health suffer. If you are disgruntled with another, remember it is your own mind which is disturbed and mental disturbances induce nervous reactions and waste power. Hence it is that a recognition of the facts of psychology has increased both our responsibility in life and our efficiency. It has shown us where the waste is and how to conserve and direct the energy. You will not be likely to run to the doctor for a pill for your irritability, or your worry habit, or your chronic selfishness You may even conclude your real complaint is not liver trouble but chronic fear, not dyspepsia but irritability, not colds but temper.

While this has to do with the conservation of energy mainly, it applies also to the development of power. In truth we have no power in ourselves: we can only regulate and adjust the instrument so that it shall be efficient, and power from above shall flow through it. This is what science does with the forces of Nature: it does not create force in any sense, it merely renders it available. If we understood ourselves as well as we understand mechanics, we could do the same with spiritual and mental forces We could admit more power, as it were, from the power-house, by enlarging the mains and making more perfect connections. An efficient will, good habits, and right-thinking imply that the mental machine is not only not wasting power, but is in a position to receive and apply a greater degree of power. We have to do with mental states, and our attitude to our own ability and to the source of our energy has everything to do with our realisation of that power. Are you praying unceasingly by concentrating upon your work?—for that sort of prayer is answered. Are you cultivating self-trust?—for that is to establish a centre of force We damn ourselves with our doubts and our faithlessness; we damn others with our lack of faith in them.

Are you cultivating any trust in God who is the energy both of your doubt and of your faith, who is the source of all power? Are you trying hopelessly to define what God is, or are you living in the divine Love and appropriating the divine Energy? Are you merely reading about the sun or are you standing in the sunshine? If you seem to lack power and strength—ask yourself these questions.

It is one of the world illusions that we have life apart from God; as if a sunbeam should imagine itself independent of the Sun, or should even deny that there was a Sun. Since all power is of God, the more we can *realise* our essential identity with God, the more we realise that power which is ours. The sense of separation weakens always. Realisation as a practical ideal has little part in the common notion of religion, and hence our religion itself is not practical, is not a working basis for daily life, but a matter of sentiment, tradition, and superstition and one hour a week is enough to devote to it. Any real means of self-help must consist in part in ridding ourselves of false concepts and establishing a normal attitude of mind and a normal relation to God, to man, and to life. We must take Psychology out of the lecture-room and bring it into practice; we must take Ethics out of the text-book and put it into right-thinking; Philosophy out of theory and put it into wisdom and self-control; and we must take Religion out of the prayer-book and put it into constant realisation of God's presence in us, for this is practical religion.

God being the source of our energy, the problem of gaining poise, or freedom, or power—the problem of self-help in other words—resolves itself into establishing a true and vital relation to God; it is a problem of realisation. Now God is Love, and to fill your heart with love, and to live in loving relation to others, is therefore to realise God to that extent and to keep the channel open to the Source. Hate, malice, selfishness close it. God is Truth, and to have true concepts is also to bring God into consciousness, and to open the channel which is obstructed by false beliefs and closed by error.

Realisation is the fruit of the inner life alone. Without meditation, without silence, without quietude it is never achieved. It is in the inner life we shall strengthen and reinforce the mind for contact with the world; it is in the inner life again that we shall seek refuge from the vanities and vexations of the world and shall renew ourselves. Therefore cultivate the silence and make it friendly to you. Relax! Stop thinking and acting to no purpose—it is a waste of power. Consider well that it does not avail how fast you run, if you are going the wrong way. Why such haste? Pause and get your bearings every day. Cease the futile effort to generate power. Go into the silence and cultivate instead an attitude of mind that will *admit* power from above.

CHAPTER VII

HEALTH

ANY practical study of psychology outside of the school room must reveal how close is the association of health and the mental states. Briefly reviewing the substance of Part II: We have seen the relation of thought to the nervous system, which may be summed up in the fact that all consciousness is motor and that every thought and feeling produces a nervous reaction. The mental state, then,—the stream of consciousness,—is the first consideration and whatever influences that has some bearing on the physical condition. We have seen that the stream of consciousness is directed or misdirected by the attention; that it is clarified by true concepts and made turbid by false beliefs; that mental states become chronic through habit and that the attendant nervous reactions must also become chronic; that undesirable pictures formed through the imaging faculty are intensified by negative emotion, and that these as well as wholesome pictures become manifest in the flesh. In considering the subconscious we have observed that normally it regulates the automatic centres; that it is interfered with by negative currents from the higher centres; that it seems to store mental pictures, and these forgotten pictures retain their power to induce nervous reactions. Lastly we have found that auto-suggestion is the efficient means of eliminating undesirable beliefs and tendencies, by infusing pure ideals and true concepts into the stream of consciousness, thus inducing healthful mental states.

To maintain such a state of mind is to invite health in the body. To think health is to aim, at least, at its embodiment; to think strength is to embody more strength. The substance of our psychology will amply refute the silly notion that merely affirming health is enough to insure health. But while mere affirmation is insufficient, it is far better than negation. It has become evident that health, no less than peace of mind, is influenced by our relation to our neighbours, as well as by our inner adjustment to life and to the external world. In other words, health is bound up with our whole moral, ethical, and religious life. For our moral, ethical, and religious concepts induce emotions or form mental pictures and these must necessarily have nervous reactions. Any defect of temperament or disposition is inimical to health. Hence the fallacy—we might even say immorality in some cases—of making no effort to overcome the moral defect which is the true cause, but merely drugging the body to remove the effect. In some instances, surely, disease is corrective, and to absolutely ignore the lesson it contains and fly to drugs, is merely an evasion and a postponement.

health is fundamentally a mental state, the result of a harmonious adjustment. Nor is this view controverted by the health of the robust but ignorant labourer. With him there is much less interference with the normal subconscious processes by the misrule of consciousness, than is usually the case with the cultivated mind and sensitive and more delicate organisation. Neither are his emotions so complex or so intense, nor his mental pictures so vivid. The sum of his conscious activity is slight, his life simple, and his compensation is a physical condition more nearly approaching that of the animal.

It is *not* contended that we can be independent of material things, but that health is a mental adjustment to these as well. What we must insist upon, as the only philosophic view, is that the material is always relative to our state of mind. We can not live without food, air, heat, but the effect of these things upon any body depends, within certain limits, upon the mind which informs that body. The same kind of food eaten during different emotive states will have different results. A given temperature is relative to our condition and the excessive heat or cold of one day is not excessive to us at another time under other conditions, or to another race of people. Sensations and impressions, be it remembered, come to us through consciousness and must therefore vary with the fluctuations of consciousness. Let it be remembered also that our beliefs concerning a thing may react upon us quite independently of the thing itself.

Mental conditions which disturb our poise or waste our power are necessarily inimical to health. Therefore right-thinking is the true basis of health, for under that condition only can the life-force utilise matter to the best advantage. Food does not give life, but the life-force must have food as building material for the body, as it must have air and water and a temperature within the limits possible to the maintenance of human life. A mind centred upon the body, too, is inimical to health. It may be accepted as a good rule that the less thought taken of the body the better. Lift the thought off the body and establish the habit of unconsciousness of this outer garment. Make it your concern to take care of the mind and let the subconscious take care of the body.

This emphasis of the importance of mental states does not imply that normal requirements are to be dispensed with. Sleep and exercise have their relation to health because, like food, they are essential. We are not to assume that because of right-thinking we can do without those things normal to physical expression. We are simply to remember that they have no relation to us independent of the state of the mind. Sleep is even more a mental than a physical rest. Exercise is a mental relaxation. From a wholly material point of view we are supposed to require such and such food in order to be well, but the awakening mind discovers this is mere opinion, and that everything, except absolute truth itself, is relative to our states of consciousness. In one part of the world or another you may see all the laws of hygiene successfully refuted by people who have never heard of them. These are for the most part man-made laws, that is, mere opinions and not laws at all. But the relation of mental states and mental pictures to nervous reactions and to health is not a man-made law but the appointed condition under which we live.

Let the aim be—"a sound mind in a sound body." This is health. It means not only a mind in harmony within itself, but a complete adjustment of the inner to the outer, and the dominion of the higher over the lower. Sensation, as we have seen, is mental. To be dominated by sensation then really means to be under the rule of a certain order of thinking. To be carnally minded means to be ruled not so much by the body as by perverted thought about the body. Causes are mental. The body is an effect—a mere appearance—changing from hour to hour and dissolved into its elements the moment the life-force ceases its connection with it.

When we *analyse* health it seems rather complex: when we *realise* health it is simple enough. It is they who do *not* sleep who know all the methods for producing sleep. The fact has become evident, however, in our analysis that health is not merely a matter of having good food, and fresh air, desirable as these may be, but has its roots deep in the soil of our mental and moral life. Health is a mental state as well as a bodily condition. We say we "feel well," but the body is incapable of feeling and it is the mind alone which feels. We must eat, but we must observe the state of mind in which we eat. We must bathe, but we must also be morally pure and mentally clean. We must exercise, but still more must we recreate and renew the mind from time to time—rid it of false and debilitating beliefs and strengthen it with truth.

Were we to begin life to-day on this basis, the problem of health and of life itself would be far simpler. But the beliefs and the mental pictures of long ago—incident perhaps to a personality we now repudiate—may still be inducing nervous reactions that disturb organic function. In addition to maintaining the integrity of the mind to-day, we must pour in pure and wholesome thought until the submerged reservoir is itself wholly pure.

We must erase the old pictures and replace them with healthful ones. We must obliterate neural paths by withdrawing the attention from the mental habits that formed them.

In a sense, however, we do begin life every day. We come into possession, as it were, of an old estate which has in all probability been mismanaged. From this hour we can manage it wisely. This day we can institute reforms which shall overcome the results of past mismanagement. Nature works for health. Thus also do love and wisdom; only false beliefs, negative emotions, and defects of character and disposition interfere and produce discord. Health is harmony, and the means of regaining a lost harmony and of maintaining it is the persistent auto-suggestion of love and truth. This does not mean the mere repetition of a truth: it means dwelling upon it until it is brought into *realisation*, and a new state of mind and a new feeling ensue. To *feel* more cheerful, kinder, and more considerate, stronger, freer, and more positive, is the result of an increased perception and realisation of truth: and to feel thus is also to have an increased bodily feeling of health.

CHAPTER VIII

DISEASE

As we have revised somewhat our idea of health, we must also revise our idea of disease. Our subject does not call for a discussion of disease from a pathologic point of view, but there is something to be said from a philosophical and psychological standpoint. Medicine has in the past disassociated disease from mental states and regarded it as if it were a thing-in-itself—an active principle to be combated, or a condition of matter to be treated by material means alone. This is less so to-day, however, than it was even ten years ago, and physicians recognise much more than ever before, not only that the mind has something to do with producing disease, but that, through suggestion, it may have something to do with curing it.

Opposed to the material fallacy to which medicine has so long committed itself, is the truth that matter does not act of itself, but is acted upon, that sensation is necessarily mental, and that disease, in place of being a principle, self-existent and co-existent with the life-force itself, is the variable expression of inner inharmony and maladjustment, the outer and visible effect of moral and mental causes. It is true that specific forms of bacteria are associated with different diseases; so are some fungi peculiar to certain trees. A microbe is no more a disease than a mushroom is a disease. It is itself a healthy organism. Decay is the soil, however, in which it grows. As mushrooms do not grow on healthy trees, neither do certain bacteria thrive in a healthy body. The atmosphere of a large city contains many kinds of bacteria. Only when they fall on the right soil do they flourish, as mushrooms only germinate when they find the right conditions.

The physician takes no account of the disease-germs in the mental atmosphere which he himself assiduously fosters, bringing his mental disease-culture from the hospital and taking it from house to house to infect the minds of his patients. The most prevalent and the most dangerous of all forms of in-disease-germs from the mind, once they get in. Thinking and talking about disease prepare the mental soil for its reception. Fear and expectancy promote its growth. Only vigorous and fearless minds, at harmony within themselves, are immune. Are you selfish, are you fearful, are you irritable? Remember these things weaken the mental fibre,—as decay weakens the tree,—and invite mental germs to lodge and develop. As the fungus thrives out of the sun, so this mental fungus is sustained in darkness and fearfulness of mind where healthy and vigorous thoughts find no nourishment.

That disease has no reality, is true in a strictly metaphysical sense: but in this sense the personality itself is unreal—the world is unreal—for neither endure, neither are permanent entities. Health and disease are merely manifestations of harmony or discord in the ever-changing body. Let us remember, however, that harmony, like light, is real and enduring, while discord and evil, like darkness, spring from no principles and have no abiding reality. We think and talk so much more of disease than of health, dwell upon it, emphasise it, that we have now infected the world-thought with the idea of disease and have made it seem more real than health. We have lost sight of the fact that health is normal and disease is largely an abnormality of consciousness.

It is entirely overlooked by most people that minor complaints would take care of themselves if we merely let them alone and did absolutely nothing but divert the attention. For it is Nature that heals, and what people really run to the doctor for is to satisfy their minds that something is being done. Nature as a recuperative force is completely ignored. The fact is overlooked again that some diseases are self-limited and, providing they do not prove fatal, run their course in a given time and stop, whether any attempt is made to cure them or not. Medicine has now come to recognise a class of nervous diseases and imaginary diseases which may be benefited by mental treatment. But all diseases are more or less nervous, inasmuch as the body is acted upon by the mind through the nervous system. Furthermore the imaging faculty has something to do with all diseases: in some cases by forming a picture of the disease; in others, as we have seen, by forming negative pictures of some sort, under stress of fright or anger, which are stored away in the subconscious and of which the patient may he wholly unaware, but which continue to induce nervous reactions that prevent the normal functions of some organ.

There are, of course, people who imagine they have complaints and who feel they are cured when the mind is disabused of the idea by which they were practically hypnotised. Their disease is primarily a diseased imagination—and that is a serious complaint. A diseased imagination is just as real as a diseased liver. Neither have reality in an absolute sense; both are real in a relative sense. Another class do not really want to be cured of their complaints. Their disease is self-love and self-pity. They are found only among those who can afford to constantly employ a doctor to lean upon. They are disinclined to make any effort to help themselves and they would rather be ill than relinquish their self-pity, which is their greatest comfort. The only cure for these people is an awakening to a new sense of life and their own responsibility in it.

While it is now admitted that functional and nervous disease may be reached by suggestion, the possibility of so reaching organic disease is still denied by physicians. It is true that in organic disease there is a lesion, a change or waste of tissue. But if the mind can waste tissue why can it not rebuild tissue? As bricks do not themselves build a wall, but the mason builds it, using bricks for material, so the mind builds the body, using food for material. In the hypnotic state, suggestion has caused a blister to appear and to disappear. Ah, little sirs, "There are more things in heaven and earth than are dreamed of in your philosophy." The life-force builds the body. If we can remove that which obstructs its activity in some direction, why should it not rebuild? A formal protest should be lodged against the term *incurable*, on the ground that it is unscientific. We may not yet have cured a certain malady, but to say that it is incurable is as absurd as it would have been a few years since to have affirmed that, because we never had constructed a flying machine, therefore flying machines were impossible; or because we never had invented a telephone, therefore telephones never would be invented. The science of Suggestion—the science of Psychology itself—is in its infancy. We have every reason to expect great developments in this direction.

There is properly no science of Medicine,

for the practice of medicine, as far as it concerns drugs, is no more than guessing. There are many excellent men in the profession earnestly devoted to helping the sick, but at best they are only guessers, and the theories and remedies of To-day will be replaced by those of To-morrow. It is well known that from the effect of a given drug upon A you can not predict its effect upon B. Neither do two schools of Medicine, nor necessarily two exponents of the same school, agree upon its use with reference to either A or B. Hence the guessing. Mark the fact that the Homeopaths refute the system of the Allopaths by using a remedy which is practically no remedy at all, so attenuated is the drug. Observe again that the majority of followers of both Mental and Christian Science are people whom medicine has failed to benefit. This is not the place to denounce or uphold any system, as such, and the author is merely an investigator in search of the facts and resolved to uphold only the facts. But the treatment of disease by suggestion in accordance with true ideals is far more scientific than the so-called science of Medicine, because it deals with causes and recognises that to remove an effect you must first remove the cause. Medicine deals with effects only and mistakes effects for cause. In this regard it is an antiquated, unscientific system and as such is destined to be replaced by the scientific use of suggestion as fast as the people see through the fallacy and outgrow it. The discontinuance of drugs—which is now well under way—does not mean the discontinuance of care, of nursing, and of some aspects of hygiene. More attention will be paid to these as less attention is paid to drugs. Still more attention will be devoted to mental conditions, mental disinfecting, and mental upbuilding. The successful physicians of the future will be practical psychologists.

To endeavour to disassociate disease from its mental and moral root and deal with the effect alone is obviously unscientific. It may be very successful in describing and diagnosing the physical effects, but it has never been and never will be successful in curing the disease, for it leaves the root untouched. Mental treatment is more exact and more scientific because it aims to remove the cause. Pain in some instances is beneficent and corrective It is a warning that certain moral defects, false beliefs, or negative tendencies, through their nervous reactions, are seriously interfering with the bodily as well as with the moral welfare. If we are wise enough to heed the lesson and overcome the error in mind, or the defect of disposition, or to erase the negative picture, the trouble will cease and pain will have served its mission. If, instead, we make no change in ourselves but simply put a drug in the stomach, we have only evaded the lesson and must continue paying the penalty, whenever occasion makes it necessary, until the lesson is learned.

In refuting the belief that disease is a roaring lion seeking whom it may devour, and affirming instead that it is an effect always of some hidden cause, we have arrived at that conclusion for which our psychology was the premise. The moral defects, the false beliefs, the tyrannous negative emotions are the real diseases, as wisdom and virtue are the real health. The ease or pain of the body is but a surface indication. Nor do the ailments of infants in the least affect our position; for children are mere weather vanes which indicate the prevailing emotive states of their parents, and are quickly upset physically, both by the inharmony and fears of elder minds and by the mental atmosphere of the household.

CHAPTER IX

MENTAL HEALING

IF we admit the facts of psychology, we must also admit the power of suggestion in the healing of disease, and that mental healing has a logical and scientific basis; for the chief aim of mental healing is the eradication of moral defects. Weakness of character, false beliefs, delusion, and discord are the seeds of disease. The physician complains that the metaphysician does not diagnose and is incapable of diagnosing the disease. The mental therapeutist does diagnose the mental and moral *causes* of disease, while from his standpoint the physician diagnoses only the *symptoms* of disease. One deals with causes, the other with effects merely. Now the metaphysician may be quite as mistaken at times in his diagnosis of causes as the physician in his diagnosis of symptoms. Human reason is never infallible, and in judging any system, allowance should be made for the limitations of its exponents. But a principle underlies the theory of mental healing, whereas there is no principle at all behind the practice of giving drugs.

The theory of mental therapeutics rests upon the great truth, which Medicine ignores, that Man is a whole in which the parts are related and interdependent. As long as there is life, the body is never detached from the mind, but all consciousness is motor, inducing nervous reactions which become manifest in the body. The superficial man—the self-as-known—is here undergoing, for some divine and inscrutable purpose, a moral and mental evolution. He was put into the world, not mainly to eat and drink, but to practise and ultimately to attain to wisdom and virtue; and in the course of this evolution his ignorance and his perversity cause him suffering of mind and body. It rests, furthermore, upon the still deeper truth that the self-as-knower—the Soul—is the real man, real because one with the eternal Knower of the universe, unchanging and unchangeable while all else passes. Harmony is the goal of life; heaven is but harmony, and harmony is a state of mind in which consciousness is in perfect accord with the Soul—that is, with God who is absolute Love and Truth. To replace the disturbed consciousness with a mind serene, uplifted, and in harmony with absolute truth, by the impression of ideals through suggestion, audible and telepathic, is the aim of the metaphysician.

Suffering, both mental and physical, has, in some cases at least, a distinctly moral significance. It points to lack of adjustment, to error and defect to be overcome, to an inharmony inimical to the general welfare. To truly heal, therefore, is not merely to patch up the body; it is to effect a moral or mental change, to eliminate factors of discord and weakness and to establish harmony. Mental healing is in fact teaching health on the basis that health is harmony—that is, a sum of moral, mental, and spiritual factors, outwardly expressed in the body. It is to instruct in the science of harmony. Suggestion is merely a means to that end.

We are not bodies: we merely have bodies, as we have clothes. Hence to live to the body as we commonly do, to centre the attention upon the body and its wants to the exclusion of the higher planes of consciousness, is a perversion for which the penalty is pain. Regeneration is a lifting of thought from the material, where it is wrongly centred, to the spiritual, where it should normally dwell. The flesh is good in its place, but it profits nothing. It is the spirit alone which avails. This is the true work of the metaphysician, if he be worthy of his difficult office. Mere hypnotic suggestion is not enough in itself—is at best only a means to an end. That end is enlightenment and moral regeneration.

Regeneration means a coming out of bondage to false beliefs and the tyranny of sensation. It means being born again, this time not of the flesh but of the Spirit: that is, into a spiritual point of view with spiritual aims—the love of righteousness and peace rather than of meat and drink. This is the normal point of view. There is first the natural man and then the spiritual man. The natural man is but the soil in which the germ of spiritual consciousness shall unfold and come to fruition. It is choked by selfishness and ignorance; it is fostered by love and truth. To admit love and truth to the mind then, by any means, is like admitting sunlight to the soil by cutting away the weeds and brush.

Regeneration means a change of heart, from vanity and vexation of spirit to serenity and peace, from selfishness and pride to love and considerateness, from dependence upon externals to a dependence upon the inner life. It is to renounce Mammon and worship God in spirit and in truth. This is the way and the life. Suffering and disappointment, and often pain and disease, turn us back into the true way from which we have strayed, or which we may never as yet have discovered in our search for happiness. Philosophy and experience both teach us the way at last, but experience is a slow teacher. It is a remarkable fact, however, that disease more than any other one cause has been instrumental in turning men from an animal existence and awakening the spiritual consciousness and a desire for the higher life.

In the process of regeneration, some aid may be required from another. The aim of the metaphysician is to arouse in you the latent capacity for helping yourself, by first eliminating the obstacles which prevent. He can put you on your feet and start you on the road. Then you must go on—no one can walk for you. To place one in a position to help himself is the greatest service one can render to another. To open your eyes to the truth, to reveal to you your own power and possibilities, and to indicate the true way of life, is the office of the mental healer, quite as much as to cure your complaints. Teach ing and healing are fundamentally related and it is only by reason of ignorance and incompetence that man has divorced them.

The metaphysician, through understanding and thought-control, develops unusual power of concentration by which his thought is brought to a focus in the mind of his patient, as a burning glass concentrates rays of sunlight. Thus he virtually focusses the light of truth upon the dark recesses of the mind, and this should set in motion the forces of that mind towards its own liberation and regeneration. This we should learn to do for ourselves as far as possible, and should only appeal to another when it seems imperative through lack of success in helping ourselves. Others may be able to see our troubles more clearly than we, having perspective and also experience in the diagnosis of mental conditions; and oftentimes a little help from another makes it possible for us to continue successfully the work for ourselves, by giving us courage and renewing our faith.

To help one to help himself, to develop his own power, come into his own estate, free himself from abnormalities and beliefs, and express perfect sanity and health in his life is the end in view. This is a doctrine of self-reliance as opposed both to the theological dogma of relying upon another to save us from the effects of sin, and the medical dogma of relying upon a prescription to free us from the effects of self-indulgence, wrong-thinking, or defects of character. It is Spartan and heroic—a creed for men and not for weaklings and milksops. It means—Play up! Play up! Play the game! Be a man! Take your punishment. Learn your lesson. Work out your own salvation; for thus and thus only come strength and understanding—yes, and compassion. While we live, let us live to some purpose; and when we die let us not die complaining. Let us aim to leave the world with the feeling that it is the better for our having lived in it and that we ourselves have made some preparation for a higher life.

Once our eyes have been opened to the subtle relation between character, disposition, prevailing mental states, and physical condition and environment, we can no longer consistently run to a doctor and say, "Cure my cold, my dyspepsia, my liver!" We may however in time of need go to the metaphysician and say: "Help me to free myself from my fears. Help me to overcome my irritability and my selfishness. Help me to a better understanding of truth and a fuller expression of love in my life." Better still we may be our own physician, administering truth to an erring consciousness, implanting true ideals, and admitting light to dark corners of the mind through the practical means of auto-suggestion. We may constantly refute error with truth, fear and worry with love and trust, disease-germs in the mind with health-thoughts. To work out salvation is to establish the habit of right-thinking, to the end that we may ultimately show forth a sound mind in a sound body.

If the road is long, be not discouraged. No brave life is ever lived in vain. Your destiny is in your own hands. To conquer one's self is the greatest of all victories. To love one another is the true law. Love is the redeemer. In the truth you shall be free. Open your heart then to love; open your mind to the truth!

CHAPTER X

CONCLUSION

IT has been assumed by some people in their enthusiasm for new ideas—to the detri ment certainly of the spread of true knowledge—that common-sense was somehow to be dispensed with. Now we shall not find any system that will take the place of common-sense, but never before has there been such good and sufficient ground for revising our notion of what *is* common-sense. To conservative and timid people, it means merely conformity to tradition. To do as our grandmothers did, they assume to be common-sense, whereas it may be only nonsense. There is no better plea for this revision than our psychology itself, which puts our whole relation to life in a new light. But it should lead us, not to ignore, but rather to substitute a true, for a spurious common-sense.

If the Idealism of the present day has shown a tendency to become extreme, it must not be overlooked that it is a reaction from the most pronounced materialism the world has ever known, and all reactions from extreme positions are liable themselves to be extreme. None the less, the present movement represents one of the most determined efforts in history to think clearly, and a noteworthy attempt of a people to free themselves from the bondage to hopeless materialism to which both medicine and theology were dooming the race. To realise the force of this movement, we have only to consider that the tenets of a hide-bound theology and of equally hide-bound schools of medicine have been modified, if ever so slightly, throughout the whole of this country by its powerful influence. While these institutions will not themselves admit this, no one who has closely observed the medical and theological straws for the past twenty years can have any doubt as to which way the wind is blowing. It is one of the great reactionary movements of history and, whereas we of the present cannot estimate its proportions for lack of perspective, future historians will so regard it.

One evidence of common-sense, surely, is to keep abreast of the times and to go with the current when, upon investigation, that current is seen to flow in the direction of the true interests of mankind and to be incident to the spiritual evolution of the race. It is another evidence of common-sense to move deliberately and, on general philosophic grounds, to avoid extremes. Theory and practice must go together in philosophy as elsewhere. We sometimes perceive the truth in sudden gleams and flashes, but by no such sudden movement is it incorporated in our whole mental life, but rather by a deliberate and evolutionary process. The propagation of truth is always checked by those emotional enthusiasts who, having become enamoured of a new theory, hasten to announce it before they are in the least able to put it into practice. Build your foundation well and your superstructure will stand; otherwise, it will surely fall, to the derision of the scoffers. A tree shall be judged by its fruits, not by what you have to say about it. Therefore be moderate in theory and assiduous in practice. Take the middle path. It is the best road for a long journey. We were not destined here to live as though we had no bodies but rather, if may be, to announce in the flesh the triumph of the Spirit.

A transition period in the evolution of

religious and philosophic thought, this is necessarily an age of fads. True growth is always from within, but fads are merely an accretion from without. In spite of the New Thought, or the Vedanta Philosophy, or Christian Science, our happiness is still a matter of wisdom and virtue and not of the beliefs we subscribe to, and we shall be judged, as heretofore, by what character we possess. Fads give rise to quacks and there are many to-day who prey on the ignorant and on the suffering—shallow individualists, medicine men, vulgarians with a show of occult learning and much self-vaunting. There are quacks in all professions and you shall know them by their pretensions. No panacea for mind or body has ever been discovered but love and truth. These are as essential to us as light and air. We have not recognised this necessity and have tried with but poor success to do with substitutes. Life is the school where we are to clarify our minds and arrive at the perception of truth, and where we are to purify our hearts and come to the realisation of love. This is never accomplished by any subterfuge, but with rich and poor, with high and low, it is a question of living and a matter of growth.

One species of modern quackery is the application of mental "treatment" to business success, and nowhere is there more room for common-sense than here. The road to true business success is honesty, intelligence, industry, and efficiency. No other road has been discovered. Some knaves get rich by stealing, but that is not a business success and their failure becomes manifest sooner or later. So-called "vibrations" calling success out of the empty air are mere incantations of witch doctors and of no more value. Such nonsense only blinds us to true methods and true ideals.

The real office of suggestion in this connection lies in helping us to help ourselves by overcoming those defects of character which inhibit or waste our power, and by arousing us to thought-control and self-trust. In this way we may be legitimately helped to business success. If poverty is the result of incompetence, it is only to be overcome by growing competent and efficient; if the result of indolence, it is corrected by industry. It is sometimes due to lack of self-trust, lack of concentration, lack of force, and often again to lack of intelligence. Whatever overcomes these deficiencies will help us to success. A prolific source of failure, and one peculiarly amenable to suggestion, is a wrong mental attitude to life and to the world—a tendency to push away the good which would naturally flow to us. If you are a victim of this tendency, if you are in the habit of standing in your own light, of denying your possibilities and affirming your weakness rather than your strength, you have it in your power to reverse the order and through systematic auto-suggestion to establish a positive and normal attitude of mind towards life. As you have pulled yourself down, now you may lift yourself up. As you help yourself, all forces conspire to help you. The quality of thought sent out is echoed back, as it were, love for love and hate for hate. Strength gathers to itself strength, as capital earns interest.

Let go of the past wherever it is interfering with your true progress. In so far as suffering is refining, uplifting, spiritualising—in so far as it is a factor in the development of character—it is good and serves the main purpose of life. But the thought that chains us to the past and interferes with our usefulness in the present is, it may be, but a form of selfishness, a mill-stone about the neck, and the sooner we disengage ourselves from it the better. Veneration for the past and for the dead ceases to be justified when it is at the expense of the present and of the living. It has been well said that our eyes were placed in the front of our heads that we might look forward and not backward.

Remind yourself ever and anon that you see life through your own mind, as through a glass, and of how much depends on the state of your mind. If the glass be out of focus the world must look awry. If the glass be clear, life will look brighter. Thus, instead of complaining of life, you will set to work to cleanse the glass and put it in focus.

It must be admitted that this is not so much common-sense as the uncommon sense which comes only to the awakening mind. But it is as natural to that state as was the self-hindering and complaining attitude to the unawakened. Our growth is an ascent and from each new vantage we get a new and broader point of view. The old point of view seemed true from the position wherein it was taken, but we have only to ascend a little way to discover our error. And in this ascent we discern, on each new plane, more and more that is truly practical as we develop and rely more upon inner forces and less upon external means. In time we come naturally to live the inner life and to place our dependence there; for once we have reached its plane, it seems as practical and as matter-of-fact as did ever the life of the senses at some lower stage of evolution.

A word to those who, while they admit the facts, find themselves temporarily unable to apply them; who realise they should control their minds but think themselves unable to do so: Every student of human nature must have observed that mental phases are common and not always to be accounted for. If you find your mind indulging in kinks of this sort, look to it that your main purpose is true—that you face the right way—but do not take yourself too seriously. All growth is uneven. If all the causes which lead to a present condition could be seen, we would understand. This being impossible, we must always take something on faith, and the more we can apply a broad view of life and of mental evolution to our particular case, the better for us. If you do not appear able to profitably direct your thought to-day, divert it in some other channel The phase will pass; to-morrow the world will wear a different face and soon you will be in possession of yourself again. Once you are, then discipline yourself against a recurrence of unfavourable conditions.

Do not overtrain mentally. It is possible to overdo anything—even virtue. A sense of humour has great saving qualities. Normal growth is better than a forced one. Above all, do not waste your energy in combating darkness. Rather open your consciousness to the light. A tranquil mind will receive the truth, as a calm lake reflects the heavens. Let tranquillity therefore be your aim. Truth is not of man but of God. You may prepare the soil, but it is God alone who gives the increase. The obstacles, however, are in man and not in God. To free ourselves from these, that the truth may enter from above and do its work, is the ideal of the Philosophy of Self-help. Ignorance, fear, passion, selfishness, all obstruct the sunlight from our mental fields and all can be removed by the salutary method of suggesting true ideals until new habits of mind and new neural paths are established. You are here to find yourself. Do not complain and talk of leaving the world because you have been burned by the purifying fire, for that is childish. But learn the lesson of your experience and see what good can be gotten from it—for often our angels come in disguise. Let nothing pass without attempting to derive some good from it.

Do not mistake anything connected with the personal self as final. Only God and the Soul are unchangeable. All else is flowing—passing phenomena and no more. It may seem to you that your habit or your disease is fixed. Not so. The kaleidoscope retains a particular form only so long as the tube is held in position: a turn of the wrist and it becomes something else. So your habits of thought have crystallised in your body and your environment and all seems enduring as a mountain. But let some intimation from the Soul come, like a gleam from above, upon the murky horizon of your thought, and the world shall appear to you in a new light. Establish a new point of view, a new and better way of thinking, and you give the kaleidoscope you call yourself another turn and a new and more beautiful combination appears in place of that old self.

Good is permanent and real; truth endures. But error has only that power we give it, the rank we accord it in consciousness. Harmony is real and self-existent; inharmony is of our own creation and dies when we cease to breathe our life into our creation. Our false beliefs objectify themselves in the phantoms we call disease to which we give reality in consciousness. Hold fast to love and truth; abide in the Spirit—for these are the realities.

It will be evident that the aim of this book is to teach harmony; to help you put yourself in tune, as if, indeed, you were an instrument, some of whose strings were in accord and others not. If life seems like a discord, it is because we are out of tune. Harmony itself is never disturbed, but a discordant instrument responds imperfectly to it. Auto-suggestion, as here presented, is merely a means of tuning the instrument; right-thinking is being in tune. Harmony itself is of God—and of the Soul which is God in us. To express harmony is to be a perfectly attuned instrument—a sound mind in a sound body.

"And be not conformed to this world: but be ye transformed by the renewing of your mind, that ye may prove what *is* that good, and acceptable, and perfect, will of God."

CPSIA information can be obtained
at www.ICGtesting.com
Printed in the USA
FSOW04n2108260217
31311FS